OLD WEST R
R CAM
Cambridge
R GRANTA
R STORT
R RODING
Newmarket Heath
Newmarket
Stetchworth
Ditton Green
Mildenhall
Barton Mills
Tuddenham
Herringswell
Cavenham
Icklingham
Ramparts Field
West Stow
Fornham St. Genevieve
Risby
Higham
Barrow
Hargrave
Bury St. Edmunds
Great Whelnetham
Bradfield Woods
Sapiston
R DOVE
Woolpit
Borley
Haughley
Rattlesden
Stowmarket
Mickfield
Debenham
Framlingham
R ALDE
Blythburgh
Walberswick
Westleton Heath
Dunwich
East Bridge
Theberton
Minsmere
Sizewell
Saxmundham
Thorpeness
The Haven
Aldeburgh
Great Glenham
Parham
Marlesford
Snape Warren
Gromford
Iken
Fromsden
Monewden
Wickham Market
Needham Market
R GIPPING
Great Blakenham
Little Blakenham
Hasketon
SANDLINGS
Sudbourne
Butley
Orford Ness
Havergate Island
Boyton
Hollesley
Shingle Street
Bawdsey
R DEBEN
Cockfield
R BRETT
Hitcham
Wattisham
Lavenham
Nedging
Offton
Flowton
Wolves Wood
Ipswich
Newbourne Springs
Brightwell
Long Melford
Haverhill
Groton Wood
Hadleigh
Belstead
Belchamp St. Paul
Sudbury
Ballingdon
Loshes Meadow
Cornard Mere
Raydon
Tattingstone
R ORWELL
Felixtowe Ferry
Trimley
Felixstowe
Shotley
R STOUR
Landguard Common
Parkeston + Harwich
Dovercourt
Crabknowe Spit
Dedham
Monningtree + Lawford
Stour + Copperas Wood
Halstead
Great Horkesley
Chalkney Wood
Ardleigh
Great Oakley
Hamford Water
Skipper's Island
Stone Point
The Naze
Walton
Frinton
R PANT
R BRAIN
R COLNE
Colchester
HOLLAND BK.
Iron Latch
Weeleyhall Wood
ROMAN R
Fingringhoe Wick
Howlands Marsh
Holland
St. Osyth
Clacton
R CHELMER
R TER
Witham
Braxted
Tiptree Heath
Oxley Meadow
Ray Island
Mersea
West Mersea
Colne Point
R CAN
Wickham Bishops
Chigborough Lakes
Maldon
Osea Island
Bradwell-on-Sea
R BLACKWATER
Dengie Marshes
0
10
MILES

Wild Flowers of East Anglia 1997
has been published
as a Limited Edition
of which this is

Number **200**

A list of original
subscribers is printed
at the back
of this book.

OVER: Common poppies at Keswick, Norwich.

WILD FLOWERS
of EAST ANGLIA

BY
STEPHEN R. MARTIN

BARON
MCMXMCVII

PUBLISHED BY BARON BIRCH
FOR QUOTES LIMITED IN 1997
AND PRODUCED BY KEY COMPOSITION,
SOUTH MIDLANDS LITHOPLATES, CHENEY & SONS,
HILLMAN PRINTERS (FROME) AND
WBC BOOK MANUFACTURERS

© Stephen R. Martin 1997

All rights reserved. No part of this publication may be reproduced, stored in a retrieval system, or transmitted, in any form or by any means, electronic, mechanical, photocopying, recording or otherwise, without the prior permission of Quotes Limited.

Any copy of this book issued by the Publisher as clothbound or as a paperback is sold subject to the condition that it shall not by way of trade or otherwise, be lent, re-sold, hired out or otherwise circulated without the Publisher's prior consent, in any form of binding or cover other than that in which it is published, and without a similar condition including this condition being imposed on a subsequent purchaser.

ISBN 0 86023 552 1

Contents

Acknowledgements	6
Introduction	8
The Lilies of the Field	13
The Flowers of the Forest	45
Wetland Wild Flowers	73
Beside the Sea	101
Breckland Blooms	119
Bibliography	136
Plant Index	137
General Index	141
Subscribers	143

ACKNOWLEDGEMENTS

East Anglia has long been noted for its accomplished naturalists, both professional and amateur, and I have received ungrudging and illuminating help over the years from so many such, and from so many of those employed by conservation bodies in the region, that there is not space to acknowledge them all individually.

However, I am delighted to thank Reg Land of the Norfolk Wildlife Trust and Peter Lawson of the Suffolk Wildlife Trust for reading the typescript and valuable suggestions for its improvement.

Dr Ian Cummings of Norwich City College was especially helpful with the chapter on woodland flowers and Martin Sanford of the Biological Records Centre at the Ipswich Museum has provided some updated Suffolk orchid information. I have benefited immeasurably in recent years from the botanical experience and expertise of the BSBI East Norfolk Recorder, Alec Bull.

Readers familiar with East Anglian floras of the two last decades will notice my pronounced and constant indebtedness to such works by Terri Tarpey & Jerry Heath, Martin Sanford, F. W. Simpson, and P. J. O. Trist, and to the rather more elderly 'Petch and Swann' Norfolk flora. These works are listed in the Bibliography and are essential aids for anyone with a developing interest in the wild flowers of East Anglia.

I am grateful to Random House UK Ltd for permission to reproduce Frances Cornford's 'The Coast: Norfolk'.

The author and publishers are particularly grateful to the County Wildlife Trusts of Norfolk and Suffolk for their valuable assistance. The County Wildlife Trusts are among the leading nature conservation bodies at county level, each responsible for an extensive range of nature reserves protecting a rich variety of wildlife. It is hoped that readers outside the Trusts will be encouraged by this book not only to visit the reserves mentioned in its pages, but also to support the Trusts' essential work in wildlife conservation by becoming members. While most people with an interest in wildlife belong to the Trust of the county in which they live, the membership rolls of the East Anglian Trusts are by no means confined to residents of the region.

For reserve handbooks, membership enquiries, and other information, contact:

Norfolk Wildlife Trust	Suffolk Wildlife Trust,
72 Cathedral Close,	Brooke House, The Green,
NORWICH, NR1 4DF	Ashbocking, IPSWICH IP6 9JY
Telephone: 01603 625540	Telephone: 01473 890089

To my wife, Angela, I owe the drawings which enhance the book and gratitude for many years' patient tolerance of my botanical obsessions and photographic excursions.

Any errors, inadequacies and infelicities remain mine.

DEDICATION

For Richard and Anna

The Coast: Norfolk

As on the highway's quiet edge
He mows the grass beside the hedge,
The old man has for company
The distant, grey, salt-smelling sea,
A poppied field, a cow and calf,
The finches on the telegraph.

Across his faded back a hone,
He slowly, slowly scythes alone
In silence of the wind-soft air,
With ladies' bedstraw everywhere
With whitened corn, and tarry poles,
And far-off gulls like risen souls.

Frances Cornford

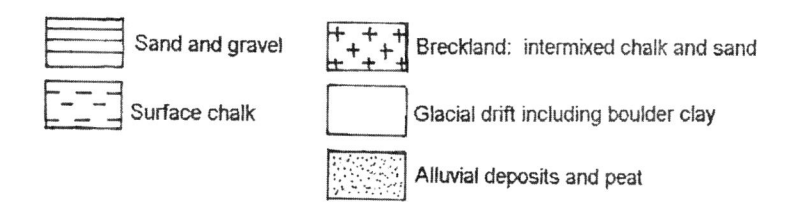

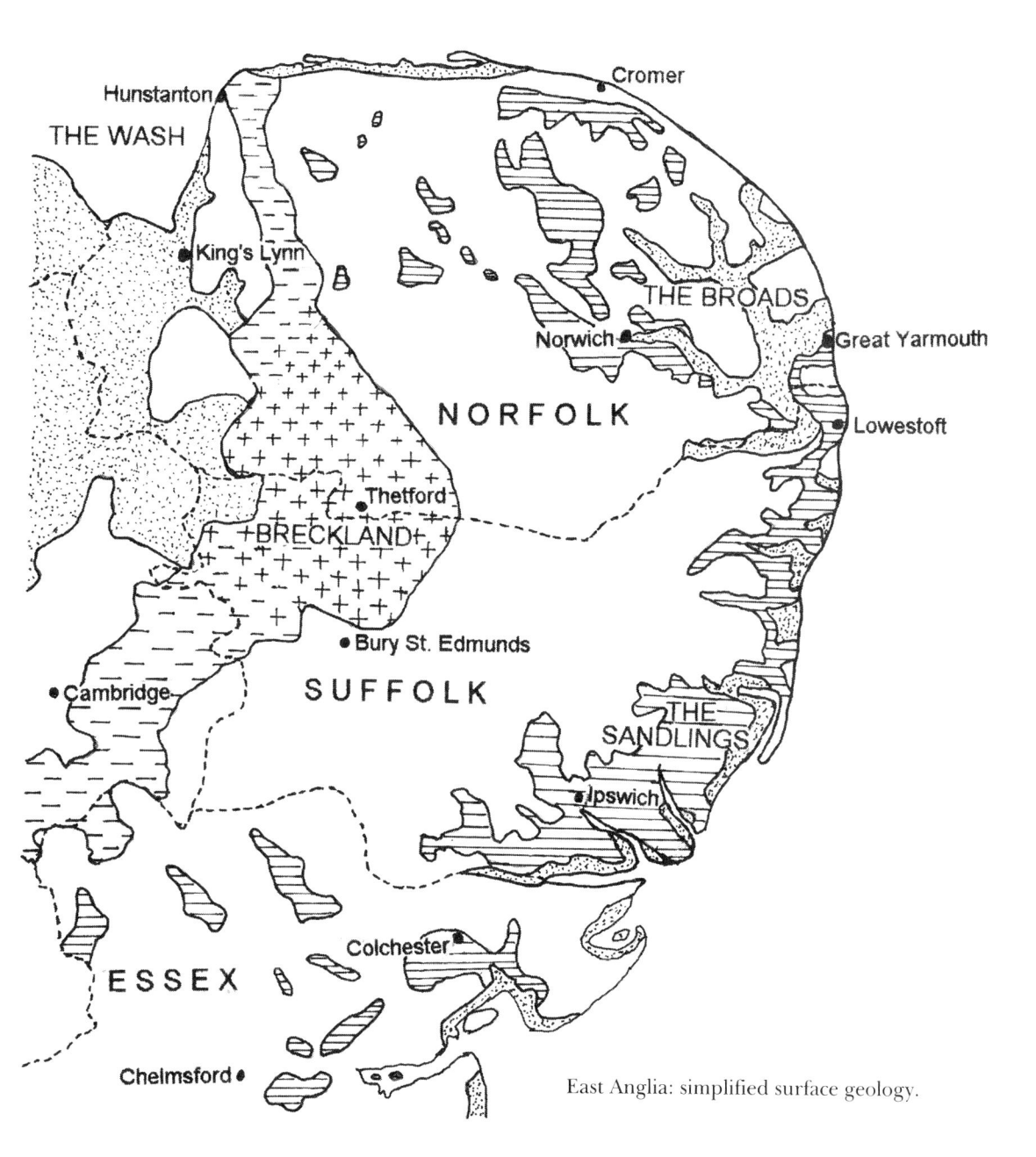

East Anglia: simplified surface geology.

INTRODUCTION

This book celebrates the richly varied wild flowers of East Anglia.

The region's diverse flora suggests an area blessed in turn with a variety of habitats and sites to confound those who are convinced, usually from afar, of its 'sameness', and, indeed, a substantial inventory of our riches is easily drawn up. East Anglia is famed for its range of wetland sites and the differing plant communities that characterise its broads, meres, fens, marshes, wet heaths, lowland bogs, wet meadows, drainage dykes and leisurely rivers. Its coastline boasts sandy and pebbly beaches, dune systems, magnificent shingle bars and spits, shellbanks, soft cliffs, and miles of wild, wonderfully-flowered estuarine and coastal saltmarshes. Inland, the extensive stretches of arable and smaller acreages of deflowered, 'improved' grassland are still punctuated and relieved by ancient broadleaved woods and considerably newer plantations, by surviving heathland, greens and commons, and even – though they are woefully reduced – by the odd flower-filled old meadow or pasture. Interesting and unusual flowers cling on along the verges and banks of lanes criss-crossing the region, and in the old, complex hedgerows still separating some fields. And there are special areas not quite like anywhere else in the kingdom, such as Breckland, with equally special plants. Here and there, occurring naturally or turned up by man's earthworks, is exposed chalk to bear another characteristic flora which again differs from the plant communities of acid sand, or wetland peat, or even of the chalky boulder-clay left after the last glaciation. Indeed, all the region really lacks, apart from significant stretches of rockbound coast, are lofty hills and the accompanying upland flowers, and the absence of abrupt declivities from towering hill to deep valley may blind the newcomer initially to the subtler variations and gradations that make up the East Anglian countryside.

So this book explores a range of wild flowers in their setting of a series of habitats occurring in East Anglia. But how does one define that region? In the end, I have concentrated on its heartland of Norfolk and Suffolk – the old Kingdom of East Anglia – and, taking advantage of the boundary lines drawn in the recent flora of north-east Essex, the part of that county which stretches south to the Blackwater and east to a north-south line through Halstead and Bradwell. But I decided also to avoid being trapped in my own corner by darting out occasionally to some fascinating eastern counties sites and species which lie just outside this chosen area.

The plants included in this book fall mainly into three categories: first, wild flowers especially characteristic of East Anglia, or particularly plentiful, or giving good shows there; second, nationally rare or scarce wild flowers that we are lucky enough to have growing in East Anglia, and species restricted in Britain to the region; and, third, wildflower species which are rare or unexpected in East Anglia, though more common in some other parts of Great Britain.

I have determinedly worked into the book any plant that I particularly like – I am sorry if I have missed any of the reader's favourites – and I acknowledge unrepentantly a bias towards flowering herbaceous plants, which are what the general reader means by 'wild flowers', over flowering shrubs and trees. Grasses, sedges and rushes are fascinating but are largely omitted. No attempt has been made to include each and every flowering herbaceous plant that grows in East Anglia. For such a catalogue, the reader should turn to the county and district floras listed in the Bibliography.

Where I know of medicinal and culinary uses of the plants, their traditional associations and significations, or their alternative common and local names – and these are interesting – they have been incorporated into the account, especially if they are connected particularly with East Anglia. For readability, I have omitted the scientific names of species from the text except where I also indicate their meaning as illuminating and as adding something to the English names, or where a species or hybrid has no English name. The scientific names of all species mentioned in the book are, however, recorded in the plant index.

Sometimes, in the discussion of the distribution of wildflower species, 'hectads' are referred to. These 10km-by-10km squares are fairly easy to discern as bounded by the bolder blue vertical and horizontal grid lines on 'Landranger' Ordnance Survey maps. Also referred to from time to time are 'tetrads', which are smaller, more popular land surface units for county plant recording and comprise squares measuring two-by-two kilometres within the larger 10km squares. There are thus 25 tetrads in each hectad. However, the reader new to such mysteries need not be deterred from reading on, for hectads and tetrads are hardly ever mentioned in a way that entails tracing them on a map to make sense of the discussion.

This book suggests selected places where the careful reader may find many of the species mentioned, though it is not a plant-twitcher's directory. I have indicated roughly where rare, endangered, or otherwise vulnerable flowers grow in the region only where this information is already freely and widely available to the general reader from other sources.

Care and sensitivity is needed when visiting reserves and other sites even in search of the less-rare plants: habitats themselves are often fragile. Trampling and 'gardening' by photographers in pursuit of a keenly sought shot can be particularly damaging, as can the quartering of, say, a fen or bog reserve by parties or even individuals. Visitors should not be blind to the well-being of the fauna when intent on viewing the flora and should do nothing to add to the danger of fire damage to vulnerable sites, especially in dry seasons.

There is free public access to most county wildlife trust reserves and to many of those administered by other conservation bodies, but where there are restrictions and prohibitions indicated in trust handbooks and other publicity material, or at the sites themselves, these are invariably in place for the good of the wildlife and must be observed. If in doubt, contact the local Wildlife Trust first.

In the case of the East Anglian county wildlife trust reserves, the name of the owning or administering trust is indicated in this book at least the first time the reserve is mentioned in each chapter, either in full or using the following abbreviations:

EWT = Essex Wildlife Trust;
NWT = Norfolk Wildlife Trust;
SWT = Suffolk Wildlife Trust.

The ownership of wildlife trust reserves is similarly indicated in the general index.

Visits to National Nature Reserves, where allowed, often require permits from English Nature, and sometimes visitors must be accompanied by a warden. Where reserves are administered by other bodies such as the National Trust, Woodland Trust, and the Royal Society for the Protection of Birds, any regulations and restrictions must similarly be observed, and it is important to approach the organisation concerned before a visit is made where there is any uncertainty as to access. Many sites referred to that are not reserves have public access, either concessionary or by right, but the mention of a site in this book implies no automatic right of access and I have indicated a number to be private in the text.

To return to the point of this book: I called it a celebration of East Anglia's wild flowers earlier, but sometimes putting it together has seemed more like writing an elegy – a lament for lost or mortally reduced species – when I have found myself so often repeating such phrases as 'now apparently extinct' or 'formerly widespread, now rare' and the like. It is painful to have to write these refrains for botanical funeral hymns and ecological dirges and it is irritating to be forced into what may seem like indulgence of the current fad of undiscriminating nostalgia. Rather, by indicating the species and habitats that have been lost and destroyed, one is in fact trying to hammer home the extent of our current impoverishment and the urgent need to try all expedients to halt it before the vibrant flowered landscape dwindles totally into what the poet Yeats called 'common greenness', and a portfolio of reserves.

There has been some progress, however, since the fashionable conservationist response was merely a blanket condemnation of the farmers for the industrialisation of farming, rather than the pinpointing and challenging of national and European agricultural policies and other factors, political, economic and social, that encouraged prairies of hedgeless monoculture, the draining of very marginal wildlife-rich wetlands, the bringing into cultivation of poorly-yielding heathland, the grubbing up of ancient woodland for arable farming or 'commercial' tree-planting, and the 'improvement' of flowery meadows to unrelieved perennial ryegrass plots. Not all farmers rushed down this path with unreflecting enthusiasm, greed, or desperate instinct for survival, and currently some attempts are being made to revive a more diverse farmscape now that a proportion of land is going out of production (though, with the dwindling of world grain reserves, 'set-aside' may prove a temporary phenomenon). Farmers themselves have set up Farming and Wildlife Advisory Groups. However, such activities to date should not be complacently overestimated either in their extent or their restorative potential. Short-term arable set-aside, for example, is arguably of limited botanical interest after the field weeds have had their day. Some conservationists stress new dangers in the botanical field such as the tendency to introduce alien strains of wild flowers which compete aggressively or hybridise with natives; others prefer to welcome the remarkable number of 'new' alien species that have become naturalised in the wild in recent years as providing some compensation for our native losses.

A host of organisations now concern themselves wholly or partly with the well-being of wildlife, including our wild flowers, and with conservation schemes and projects. Nationally, English Nature watches over National Nature Reserves, designates Sites of Special Scientific Interest and funds conservation activities by other bodies. The Countryside Commission, National Trust, National Rivers Authority, Forestry Commission, the water companies and even the Ministry of Agriculture, despite or because of changes to their remits and sometimes their names, have all given increased attention to conservation matters in recent years, albeit some more wholeheartedly and effectively than others. At county level, the East Anglian wildlife trusts lead the way in administering reserves and conservation schemes, cooperating with other bodies, including local and county councils, acquiring support from business and industry and overseeing activities by local groups of conservation volunteers and young people. County and local natural history societies gather invaluable data on the status of our wildflowers, as does the Botanical Society of the British Isles, which gives increasing attention to conservation matters. The Wild Flower Society encourages a wider public interest in plants and the rapidly-expanding Plantlife organisation works specifically for wildflower conservation by acquiring reserves and instigating programmes to conserve threatened species. The Woodland Trust plants new broadleaved woods as well as protecting flower-filled ancient ones.

The very existence of this multiplicity of bodies with a principal or subsidiary conservationist brief or function – bewildering, one imagines, to the reader with a new interest in wild flowers and their habitats – is perhaps the most eloquent proof of the threat to our wildflower sites and the depleted state of our native flora. It is vital and encouraging that conservation bodies exist, but saddening in a way that they need to in such numbers, and have to be such untiring fighters, if our flowers are not to dwindle further.

But why bother? Apart from the little matter of human survival being tied to our planet's ecological health, we can advance various arguments for floral diversity, stressing for instance the need to facilitate scientific study or to ensure that the botanical gene bank is fully available for human medical and nutritional applications. But our delight in wild flowers is surely more spontaneous and heartfelt than this, and we should not be embarrassed to assert the 'splendour in the grass' and 'glory in the flower' as being, to us, an end in itself. As members of a diverse species ourselves, infinitely adaptable to a strange variety of habitats, activities and occupations, it satisfies and reassures us at profound levels of being to be surrounded by a complementary wildlife diversity. And rich, intricate, interdependent and evolving wildlife communities seem to validate our own social complexity. Wild, but never alien (except sometimes in the narrow botanical sense of the word), the flowers surrounding and even penetrating our towns and villages are bound into our history, customs, and affections, and we do indeed retain a need to celebrate their beauty and variety, despite the losses.

LEFT: Parts of a typical flower and RIGHT: Parts of a typical orchid flower.

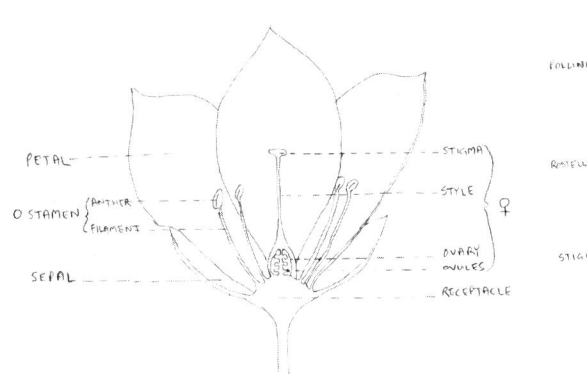

Usually, a flower comprises male and female reproductive organs surrounded by a perianth of sepals and petals. The sepals are known collectively as the calyx and the petals as the corolla. Flowers, however, vary enormously in form and some parts of the typical, imaginery flower shown here are modified in, or even occasionally absent from flowers of many actual species. As an example of a considerable degree of modification, see the orchid flower.

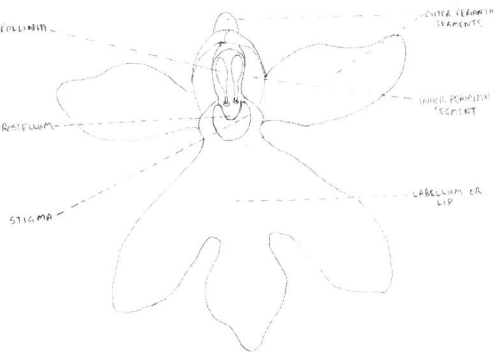

Here the perianth consists not of the regular whorls of green sepals and coloured petals of the typical flower, but rather three outer and three inner perianth segments. The most prominent inner segment is the labellum or lip, which often includes a backward-projecting spur containing nectar to attract pollinating insects. The sexual organs are also modified: the stamens are reduced to one in all native East Anglian orchids, this one stamen being divided into two pollinia. There are three stigmas: two fertile and one, the rostellum, infertile.

LEFT: Dyer's greenweed. RIGHT: Corn marigold.

THE LILIES OF THE FIELD

> Be she fairer than the day,
> Or the flow'ry meads in May;
> If she think not well of me,
> What care I how fair she be?
> George Wither

A flowery meadow, it seems, best exemplifies the fairness of the countryside in the public imagination. Or at least, those with something to sell think so, judging from the stream of advertisements in which shampooed beauties, frolicking children or carefree lovers appear among the buttercups. I use 'public imagination' advisedly, for younger East Anglians may well have never set eyes on such meadows, or at best seen them only rarely as isolated or preserved relics of the past. Only in a few favoured, special places in Britain – such as Upper Teesdale with its famed northern hay meadows – do such flower-filled fields now form part of the living tapestry of the landscape in a quantity and of a quality commensurate with our cherished imaginings. Nationally, we are said to have lost at least 95% of our old hay meadows to the plough, to rye-grass re-seeding inimical to floral richness, and to other appropriations or sheer scrub-creating neglect. By 1986, 85% of all grassland in lowland Britain had been damaged by fertilisers and Suffolk, as a sad example, is said to retain only a fraction over 1% of its former unimproved grassland of notable conservation value. East Anglia's loss of species-rich grassland to arable has been particularly grievous, but you may be hard-pressed now even in western pastoral counties to find many other hues freckling the lowland green.

We should not, of course, think of our few surviving meadows as 'natural grassland', but as a managed wildflower habitat created over the centuries by grazing farm animals, traditional haymaking and a regime in which spraying was unknown and soil fertility was not dramatically increased, for nothing was applied but dung or, in meadows subject to flooding, silt. Such practices and refrainments created a varied sward in which the slow-growing and delicate wildflowers and grasses were not dominated and choked out by more coarse and luxuriant species. And the lie of the land and nature of the soil were generally allowed to determine the constituent species of the sward, so that, for instance, wet-loving marsh marigold and lady's-smock could grace the undrained damper fields and a host of lime-lovers brighten meadows on base-rich soils.

In much of our region, meadows and old pastures remain only as nature reserves, horse paddocks and grazed or infrequently-mown greens and open commons. Permanent pasture even at its best never quite rivalled the floral richness of a hay meadow, and through the post-war years most grassy fields became 'improved' pastures which were sprayed with fertilisers to encourage grasses and with herbicides to discourage clovers and other broad-leaved plants, or were merely leys; that is, ploughed fields seeded with grass for silage.

Some landowners preserved a few acres or odd corners from intensive arable farming, though it is faith misplaced to set aside an arable patch – or indeed a large acreage of official 'set-aside' – and expect it to become flower-rich grassland spontaneously. As Oliver Rackham has said, to re-create a historic grassland we would probably need to live to the age of 200. Since fair odds could be obtained against this eventuality, our better hope is to take his implication that it is more realistic – and increasingly urgent – to ensure that those meadows and old pastures which do remain are saved, so that grazing cows with mouthfuls of flowers and the scent of new-mown hay are not wholly relegated to the realm of sentimental recollection.

Of course, sowing or planting flowers and grasses to create within a couple of decades an approximation to old grassland – a 'facsimile' as it has been called – is worthwhile so long as we are clear that we are not recreating what has been lost, and are vigilant lest, ironically, we provide the excuse of the destruction of more ancient flowery fields on the grounds that the new contrived grasslands compensate for and replace them. There has been a noticeable burgeoning in recent years of introductions of wildflowers to private gardens and such public places as road embankments, derelict land and amenity grassland. This again is encouraging, but can bring its own problems: the Wildflower Seeds Working Group has drawn attention to the dangers of foreign seed present in some wildflower mixes offered for sale, which can give rise to plants different from the native forms. These may threaten biodiversity and ecological balance by crossing with those native forms, effectively eliminating their genetic distinctness. Birdsfoot trefoil, kidney vetch, ox-eye daisy, sainfoin and salad burnet can all be seen in vigorous 'foreign' forms already, but the group has evolved an accreditation scheme for seed suppliers to ensure only native seeds are sold, and the Botanical Society of the British Isles already distributes a leaflet, *Wild Flower Plants and Seeds*, giving guidance on which species are suitable for introduction into wildflower gardens and landscaped areas, and listing suppliers of seed derived only from stock of wild British origin. A National Seed Bank has also been set up so that any plant becoming extinct in the wild can in effect be brought back from the dead and reintroduced. Spiked speedwell from Norfolk's Weeting Heath is an early donor. Another hopeful area is former heathland that becomes long-term 'set-aside' under the new agricultural dispensation. The Norfolk Wildlife Trust has already drawn up management plans for landowners wishing to restore land in this way, though this is, almost literally, new ground, and who knows how near to the old heathland we can get?

'The field', historically, could mean simply the open countryside as opposed to wooded land. So this chapter can include unblushingly some of the 'lilies' not only of meadow and pasture, but also those that are more likely to be found in East Anglia on other forms of grassland or, driven from former habitats, on grassy refuges such as churchyards and wayside verges. We must also not forget such flowers of the arable fields and field margins as have resisted extinction by modern farming methods.

Now that even golden buttercup meadows are hard to find, grassland flowers that never graced every parish even in the most favourable times and conditions are rarities indeed. One such plant we are lucky to possess in East Anglia is the fritillary or snakeshead. I prefer the running together of the two common names as 'snakeshead fritillary' because I like both, and the compound has the justification of distinguishing this perennial plant from the many other fritillary species, though admittedly those others do not grow in the wild in Britain. Other names for the plant are 'chequered lily', 'leopard's lily', 'guinea-hen flower', 'pheasant's lily' and 'snakeshead lily': you takes your pick.

The scientific name, *Fritillaria meleagris*, describes in both its parts the marking of the flowers. *Fritillaria* is from the Latin *fritillus* 'a dice box' and *meleagris* means 'speckled' or 'spotted' (it is the Greek for a Guinea hen). Both elements represent attempts to describe the chequerboard or scaly patterning of the petals in reddish and brownish purple, lilac-pink, and all the indescribable shades between. These scales justify the 'snakeshead' appellation, but one needs to see the flowerheads a day or two before their opening to appreciate fully the justice of the name. Fully open flowers hang down almost like bells from their shepherd's-crook upper stems, each with a clapper-sheaf of bright yellow stamens. The buds on the verge of bursting open, truly of snakeshead shape, similarly hang from their slender stems, but often with snout thrust slightly outwards from the vertical, as if in the process of rising up to strike. Their reptilian connotations and rather unassertive appearance in the mass among the grasses and brighter flowers of an open meadow have led some to see them as sullen, sulky, sombre, even sinister flowers and Richard Mabey has unearthed local names in other parts of England associating them with death, disease and other unpleasantnesses: dead-men's bells, lepers' lilies, toad-heads and frogcups. And there are more: crowcup, bloody-warrior, death-bell and the Lazarus-bell. And, depending on the locality, they may be drooping-, mournful-, or solemn bells of Sodom, or doleful bells of sorrow! The plant contains the alkaloid Imperialine, and is indeed poisonous, but it is as easy to concentrate instead on the fritillary's poise and grace and appreciate the delicate creamy-white variant that occurs quite commonly within large populations to counteract any sultriness in the type plant.

Current botanical opinion designates the fritillary a native perennial plant. It grows now in numbers only in the Thames Valley and Suffolk, in damp meadows and pastures, preferring fields grazed after haymaking. It was once recorded in pastures near Harleston, but is now extinct there. Before 1950, you could have found it in a dozen Suffolk parishes in river-valley meadows, pastures and marshes, but several sites have been lost since to drainage and 'reclamation' and it is said that only four now remain, though *Source Plants in Britain* records it in eight Suffolk tetrads and one Norfolk tetrad since 1970. It has recently appeared in Norfolk, almost certainly introduced, at Holt. To be sure of seeing fritillaries, visit one of the Suffolk Wildlife Trust reserves sheltering the species. The most famous, with the country's largest population of over 300,000 plants growing in poorly-drained, alkaline conditions, is undoubtedly the six-acre Fox Fritillary Meadow, near a tributary of the Deben in the Framsden district. We owe its preservation to the Fox family, in particular Mrs Queenie Fox, who showed both a conservationist's instincts and a grasp of applied psychology when she defused their collecting urge by allowing visitors each to pick a single fritillary bloom. Though the meadow was bought by the Trust in 1976, you must still make yourself known to the farmer and sign the visitors book when you visit the meadow today – but the number of visitors has so grown, and the prospect for wildflower survival so worsened, that there can be no picking now. It is practically unknown for the plant to colonise new sites, as, despite seed production commonly of a hundred or so seeds per capsule, it normally increases only by vegetative reproduction of the bulb, as do a number of haymeadow plants. A fritillary problem not down to human beings is the propensity of visiting birds – pheasants in the main – to peck large numbers of the flowerheads ragged. Bird-scarers do not seem to solve the problem, but may alleviate it.

A few fritillaries also grow at the SWT Martins' Meadow, near Monewden, not far from the Fox Meadow, but a better show is usually to be found at Mickfield Meadow, a little to the west between Debenham and the A140 road. This was Suffolk's first nature reserve, bought in the nick of time to prevent the old wet grazing meadow on sandy clay loam from being ploughed up. It is an interesting case in that scrub came to dominate the field for many years and only a handful of fritillaries continued to bloom in a small clearing. But since the scrub was bulldozed away in the 1970s, the fritillaries have reappeared with a vengeance, even though a large, luxuriant patch of wood anemones flourishes towards one corner, apparently undismayed by the lack of tree-cover. Other good plants at Mickfield include the umbellifer, pepper saxifrage, lots of lady's-smock, and goldilocks buttercup.

Mickfield demonstrates the embattled condition of our remaining wildlife sites. As one drives towards it from the village whose name it bears, the clustered buildings, trees, churchyard and small, hedged, grassy fields give way suddenly to stark intensive arable: large, hedgeless fields of which one can hardly see the far boundaries and a borderless concrete track running across the prairie. The meadow itself is a vulnerable rectangle or wedge of less than two hectares stockaded behind tall hedges, lying shallowly cupped in the surrounding arable so it seems that the fertiliser run-off must surely have undermined and penetrated its slender defences and done irreparable harm. But no, the stile giving access through the tall hedges delivers one suddenly into an oasis full of life's juice.

Go to Mickfield also to enjoy the cowslips in May. So rarely, now *Primula veris* has been forced mainly onto grassy verges, does one see it spread generously over the spacious surface of a damp meadow. This is not to say that it grows in a continuous sheet at Mickfield, in jam-packed profusion like buttercups in an old pasture: that is not the way of cowslips. Some might think their egg-yolk brightness threatens to dazzle out the sober subtleties of the fritillaries, but surely one is grateful to see the two species intermingling in such good heart.

Cowslips are still quite common in our region, chiefly on chalk and boulder-clay, but you will rarely find them in woods, except in very open, grassy glades. They are rare in Breckland and are landlubbers, avoiding growing within smelling-distance of the sea. Unlike fritillaries, you are bound to see them on grassy, usually treeless roadside verges and field margins on a drive of any length through East Anglia, proclaiming the firm establishment of spring (*veris* means 'of spring').

Cowslips are also known as paigles – or peggles in some parts of Norfolk – possibly from 'to peggle', meaning to hang and shake like a cow's neck! There is disagreement about the derivation of 'cowslip' itself. Some have argued that the wrinkled leaves are like a cow's lips or a preparation of a calf's stomach used as rennet and called keslop in Yorkshire. Interestingly, lady's bedstraw, certainly used in time gone by to curdle milk, is sometimes called keeslip in Scotland. Perhaps more likely is the proposition that the cowslip's name comes from Old English *caslyppe* ('cow-slop' or '-slime'), from the plant's tendency to grow where cow-pats are found, and cowslop is in fact an old Norfolk variant of cowslip. This, of course, could simply mean it often occurred in grazing meadows and pastures; it need not imply that the pats themselves created the conditions favourable to cowslip growth.

That a wine may be made from cowslip flowers is widely known: cowslip wine would probably be mentioned second only to elderberry if the traditional average man on the Clapham bus were to be asked to come up with the names of English home-made country wines. It cures insomnia – but which wine doesn't? – and has been used to treat jaundice and measles. A vinegar may also be made from the cowslip. You can use the chopped rhizome to make a tea, or chop the leaves and boil them in water, then leave the brew to stand before taking it to relieve catarrh. The plant also had any number of other names, uses and associations. It has been known as herb-Peter or St Peter's keys-of-heaven; it has been called palsy-wort because it allegedly cures that ailment, as it also supposedly cures migraine and calms the nerves. Children suck the flowers for their sweetness and in Cambridgeshire, and widely elsewhere in the country, there was a tradition of compressing the flowers to make 'paigle-balls' used to divine the kind of lover one would have or, more grimly, to predict the length of one's life or place of death. Not far north, in Lincolnshire, cowslips were scattered at the foot of the maypole, adding an underlying fertility-symbol significance to the many indications of this plant's immemorial part in the common-day life of England.

One final curiosity: an old belief has it that replanting a cowslip upside down induces it to produce red flowers. Presumably this unlikely conviction was a way of accounting for the occasional reddish variant growing in the wild and we ought not to assume too readily that all such colour-forms we may find result from crossings with garden polyanthus.

When visiting Mickfield in spring you may notice a plant with leaves reminiscent of a large plantain, but showing you nothing by way of a flower. This is meadow saffron, which grows at Mickfield in small numbers. The corms apparently were transferred from a meadow at Ashbocking more richly endowed with the species, when it was destroyed by ploughing. It also occurs in small numbers in the SWT meadow reserve at High House, Monewden. But the best place to see it is in First Church Meadow at the Martin's Meadows reserve, again near Monewden, though the display in the last few seasons has been a mite disappointing, in contrast to the gloriously abundant display when I visited the meadow in the blazing August of 1990. But perhaps it is all a matter of timing: the specific element of the plant's scientific name, *Colchium autumnale*, accurately indicates the fact that one can see the flowers in normal seasons in late August and through September, but, impatient for my annual 'fix', I have been unable to resist mid-August visits to Martin's Meadows.

The clusters of crocus-like flowers, ranging in colour from purplish- and lilac-pink through to warmer, glowing pinks, with some pure white plants, rise ravishingly from the aftermath just as it seems summer has burned all virtue and sucked all freshness from the earth. But, of course, the flowers are formed in their corms before any high-summer droughts.

Because the leaves die down and disappear in July before the blushing flowers emerge, the alternative name of naked ladies was coined in the 17th century and in Norfolk they have been known as naked boys. In various other parts of England the plants are naked Jacks, -men, -nannies, -virgins or -maidens, and the Germans, less delicately and more unappealingly, call meadow saffron *nakenhure*, naked whore. But it is also often called, confusingly, the autumn crocus. Certainly it looks much like a crocus, though it is distinguished from the true crocuses by having six stamens rather than their three. The real autumn crocus, naturalised here and there in England and Wales, is *Crocus nudiflorus*. Confusion with another crocus also sometimes occurs: our plant may be meadow saffron, but it is not the 'true' saffron crocus, *Crocus sativus*, once cultivated in England for culinary purposes (the yellow food dye and spice derived from its stigmas), particularly in Cornwall, Wiltshire and, of course, near Saffron Walden in Essex. The colchicums derive the name of their genus from the old Colchis, now in part Georgia, to the immediate south of the Cauceses, where some species are apparently common. Our species contains a toxic alkaloid, colchicine, which can be fatal in large doses, but the corms have been used sparingly to relieve the discomfort of gout and as a more general painkiller. However, it is a dangerous plant that should not be used in the house and it is odd that the meadow saffron was ever tolerated in grazing meadows, for it is toxic also to young cattle.

The fritillary is included as an East Anglian plant because Suffolk is one of its few strongholds: I must admit to including the meadow saffron because it is instead a rare but beautiful interloper in our region from its preferred wetter, milder home ground in the west, especially around the Severn Estuary. It was thought to be extinct in Norfolk until a well-established colony in the grassy grounds of a large private house at Thelveton came to public notice. In Suffolk, it is now very local, though it was formerly found in some 13 parishes.

Like Mickfield, Martin's Meadows are exceptionally beautiful in the spring with cowslips and fritillaries, but additional delights are provided a little later by the ox-eye daisies and the yellow rattle (also known as rattle basket in Norfolk), and by the green-winged orchids which follow the early-purple orchids. If you take the trouble to circumambulate High Church Meadow, you may find a white form of the early-purple if the plant is obliging in the year of your visit, and I have also seen pale flowers covered with faint mauve flecks at the Norfolk Wildlife Trust's Honeypot Wood reserve in Norfolk. *Orchis mascula* normally ranges from full-blooded red-purple, through reddish hues (it was called red Robin in Essex) to various pink shades, and is indeed the male orchid because vigorously red or reddish flowers were traditionally thus distinguished from delicate 'feminine' blue ones: so much for the universality of 'blue for a boy'. The early-purple has other strong masculine associations and *orchis* means 'testicle', referring to the pale double tubers of many of the family, which in the case of the early-purple have been used in love potions, though its additional small, shrivelled tuber of the previous year was considered feminine! The Queen, in Act IV of *Hamlet*, refers to:

> ...long purples
> That liberal shepherds give a grosser name,
> But our cold maids do dead men's fingers call them.

One such name was rampant widow, but local masculine names can be more unblushingly 'gross': priest's pintle, cullions and cods are a sample. The flower itself has a strong tom-cat scent. The early-purple orchid is now more characteristic of our coppiced broadleaved woods, often on the boulder clay, than grassland sites such as Martin's Meadows.

One quick and easy way of distinguishing the early-purple from the green-winged orchids at Martin's Meadows is to glance at their leaves, which are almost invariably blotched with purple, probably the source of one of the early-purple's local names, the blue butcher. This is almost certainly a polite emendation of the original bloody butcher, deriving from the dark 'spots of blood' on the leaves. Attempts to claim the plant for Christianity can be seen in the tradition that the blotches represent Jesus' blood which dripped from the cross. Though the green-winged orchid also has flower spikes of various colours from blackish-purple or purple-violet through reddish, lilac and pink shades to pure white, the blue-green leaves are never spotted and it is often dumpier than the early-purple. It usually has green, or occasionally bronzy, veins as parallel lines on the two lateral sepals of the flower, hence its name: an East Anglian alternative is the green-veined orchid and elsewhere it is known as bloody-man's finger and goosey-gander. It never grows in old woodland, though scrub sometimes overgrows it on neglected grassland, as it did for some 30 years at the Essex Wildlife Trust's Iron Latch Meadow north-west of Colchester, until an eight-year clearance programme induced a steady recovery and increase in the numbers of flowering spikes.

A common or meadow covered in green-winged orchids in May and early June is a wonderful sight, as it often still grows in large numbers despite an overall rapid decline owing to habitat loss. *Scarce Plants in Britain* suggests it is not yet scarce nationally, but warns that its map showing the species extant in many East Anglian hectads masks a great diminution of the numbers of sites within those squares. Good north-east Essex EWT sites

ABOVE: Snakeshead fritillaries, Mickfield Meadow, Suffolk, on May Day. LEFT: Churchyard flowers at St Mary's, Shotesham, including pyramidal orchids, ox-eye daisies and bird's-eye trefoil. RIGHT: Meadow saffron at High House, Monewden, Suffolk, in late August. BELOW: Sulphur clover by the roadside at Topcroft, Norfolk.

include Oxley Meadow and, just outside our region, Hitchcock's Meadows, Danbury, where the rare autumn lady's-tresses orchid is also found. In Suffolk, try the SWT reserves at High House, Monewden and Winks Meadow, Metfield (worth visiting for the buttercups alone), and the species grows also in meadows at Hasketon and at Chippenhall Green. It is found now almost exclusively on boulder clay sites of central and north-eastern Suffolk, though there is a curious exception on peaty sand at Wilde Street, Mildenhall. In Norfolk, the best sites are the NWT New Buckenham Common and Hoe Rough reserves and various other south Norfolk greens and commons, including Boyland Common north of Shelfhanger, and Gissing Common for the white form. There are still one or two private grassland sites with an abundance of the green-winged orchid, but these must remain undivulged.

A curiosity of Martin's Meadows is the old double garden daffodil, *Narcissus van Sion*, which was apparently a favourite plant of the Garnham family who farmed at Monewden before 1899. The small broom, dyer's greenweed, which is rarish now in Norfolk, Suffolk and north-east Essex, grows at the edge of the meadow. As its name indicates, it was gathered by dyers as the source of a yellow dye which was mixed with the blue from woad to make, predictably enough, a green dye. In East Anglia, it was often simply the green- or greening-weed.

The delightful Winks Meadow, on boulder clay, is the home of another much rarer orchid of our region. Some 15 flowering frog-orchid plants were found there in 1990 during the Suffolk Orchid Survey – the first Suffolk record for 30 years. There are currently no known remaining sites in Essex and Norfolk, though the frog still grows at one place in Cambridgeshire. Winks Meadow was sheep-grazed before World War II and local memory and tradition have it that it has never been ploughed: Simpson has argued that the ploughing of old horse-pastures with the coming of tractors probably accounted in large part for the frog's decline in Suffolk. One thinks of it now as more a species of north and upland Britain, where it can grow on rock-ledges as well as the edges of woods and in dune slacks. It is a 'green' orchid like the bog and fen orchids, though, like the man orchid, it sometimes displays in its small flowers and upper stem a reddish brown (or, in the frog's case, sometimes purplish-brown) tinge, particularly in those plants on sites with very sunny aspects. In exposed positions, frog orchids can be only 5cm high, and I have had to search for them on my knees in Hebridean *machair* grassland, but lowland or southern plants are often taller and can reach 35cm. The flowers are slightly honey-scented (some say honeysuckle), but it is difficult to persuade oneself of any resemblance to, or discover any other connection with, a frog.

Old chalk grassland is one of the richest of wildflower habitats. But although chalk underlies much of East Anglia, it appears at the surface only in the west. Even where it is found, much of the former grassland has been lost to arable. Counties in other regions – Kent, for example – held on to most of their chalk downland until the post-war years partly because the valley-sides were too steep to plough, but the East Anglian topography offers little such protection. The dry valley of Ringstead Downs in north-west Norfolk is in fact so untypical of our region in its similarity to more southerly chalk downlands that one could almost believe it must have been artificially gouged out of the surrounding countryside as a startlingly ambitious country-park project. But its sunny, south-facing slopes (be sure to penetrate to them beyond the central arable section if your approach to the NWT reserve is from the Ringstead Village end) are fragrant with thyme in summer, among yellow rock-roses and pale-pink or white squinancywort. If you sit to admire these small carpeters, beware of a sudden involuntary rise caused by the spiny basal rosette of leaves of the dreaded 'picknickers' peril', the stemless or dwarf thistle. The quaint name squinancywort comes from the plant's 18th-century use in healing tonsillitis or 'squinancy' (quinsy), when made into an astringent gargle. The related second element of the scientific name, *Asperula cynanchia*, means 'dog-throttle' and was the Greek word for quinsy. It is nowadays a fairly scarce plant in East Anglia. Nor is the rock-rose getting any more common, and it is probably extinct now in East Suffolk, though it did turn up apparently for the first time in north-east Essex in 1988 on a roadside verge near Pentlow. It is a *Helianthemum*, which means 'sun-lover', and cultivars are of course popular rock-garden plants for a dry, sunny site.

In 1968, the year of publication of the *Flora of Norfolk*, the authors could still write of chalk grassland maintained by grazing around Caldecote and Marham Fens, at Lambs Common, East Walton Common and the drained Beachamwell Fen, and as forming large parts of Foulden Common. In Suffolk, old chalk grassland was once widespread between Bury St Edmunds and Newmarket (there are old records for long-gone early spider and burnt orchids in the Bury area), and sheep were extensively grazed. Old, dry downland-type grassland with a chalk flora survives as Newmarket Heath, half of which is in Cambridgeshire. The Breckland heaths also boast types of chalk grassland, but deserve separate treatment in the last chapter as part of a wildflower area unique in Britain. In north-east Essex there are a few patches of chalk at the surface near Sudbury.

You will have to search more diligently now than when 'Petch and Swann' was published for the remaining chalk grassland sites and scraps, but man-made pits and embankments often repay examination, as they sometimes penetrate to the chalk beneath, or the banks are constructed of chalk, dug from the accompanying ditches or sometimes from nearby borrow-pits. And they need not always be ancient to carry a most acceptably diverse flora: Narborough Railway Line, one mile south of the village of the same name in west Norfolk, and a Norfolk Wildlife Trust reserve, is a disused railway embankment raised in the 19th century which now carries little other than an array of shrubs, grasses, chalk flowers, birds, butterflies and botanists.

The dull-purple autumn gentian flowers at Narborough from July onwards along with the silky-yellow kidney vetch, known sometimes in East Anglia as ladies' fingers and in Norfolk – delightfully – as luck: you were certainly considered lucky to find it if you needed treatment for a cut. Look also for the small scabious (the rough leaves of some scabious species were said to cure scabies), and ploughman's spikenard, *Inula conyza*. This last gets its common name from being a kind of poor-man's version of the scent-yielding true spikenard from India, for it has an aromatic root which possibly the plough might turn up. *Inula* may lead back tortuously via elecampane and its old name, *Helenium*, to Helen of Troy, and *conyza*, it is said, may come from the Greek *konis*, dust, as moths and other insects were kept at a distance by the use of a powder made from the dried leaves. Two other plants at Narborough long assumed to have medicinal virtue are eyebright, from which, when dried, were produced infusions and lotions that were thought not only to brighten the eye but also actually to cure eye troubles up to and including blindness (its scientific generic name, *Euphrasia*, comes from the Greek for 'delight'), and the little white fairy flax, *Linum catharticum*, which is fairy-like in that it is much more delicate and tiny than the blue species of flax, though the name may imply simply a traditional connection with fairies. Its other name, purging flax, translates *catharticum* and obviously indicates its efficacy as a purgative.

The perky little blue-and-white milkwort was thought to stimulate milk secretion in nursing mothers and to increase the yields of cows which grazed it. It is sometimes used in cough mixtures.

All these chalk grassland plants, together with the butterflies they attract, delight the eye at Narborough from about midsummer onwards. But delay a visit until July to breathe to full effect the mingled fragrances of wild thyme and the taller, purpler marjoram, one of the more unusual applications of which was the provision of strengthening baths for weakly children. Essence of marjoram is used for colognes and for scenting soap. These two plants grow in unusual plenty here, though at least some of the species mentioned as established at Narborough grow also on the other remaining chalk grassland sites in our region, usually with a speciality or two not to be found at the Norfolk site.

As for further old railway chalk grassland sites in East Anglia, there is a cutting in Suffolk north of Haughley Junction which has the regionally rare yellow-wort, whose flowers seem to close invariably after lunchtime, and there are other good banks in cuttings through the chalk between Bury St Edmunds and Higham.

The other, more ancient refuges for these grassland plants are the earthworks of the chalky parts of our region. One thinks particularly of the various Devil's ditches or dykes: the Suffolk Black Ditches crossing Cavenham Heath to Icklingham and between Risby and Cavenham; and, in Norfolk, the Devil's Ditches between Cranwich and Weeting and, almost obliterated, the Narborough – Beachamwell earthwork. There is also the earthwork at Garboldisham where the blue spires of spiked speedwell rise, alas, no more, though reintroduction of the species has been attempted at nearby East and West Harling Heath. There are also, more rarely, the non-linear earthworks such as the still-impressive Warham Camp not far south of Wells in north Norfolk, with its colourful concentric circles of ditches and herb-rich banks, like some floral catherine wheel after midsummer. There is public access to this delightful private site, but avoid disturbing grazing cattle and watch out for cowpats, even on the banks themselves! As for disused chalk-pits, we should not forget that it is one of these near Mildenhall that one of the region's greatest floral treasures, the military orchid, grows.

We must ignore the county boundary across Newmarket Heath and step from Suffolk into Cambridgeshire for a moment if we are to enjoy the flowers of the great Devil's Ditch, an early Saxon defensive fortification which crosses the Heath and racecourses on its seven-and-a-half mile way from Reach to Ditton Green, near Stetchworth. On the grassland before one reaches the embankment, the clustered bellflower with its deep violet flowerheads may be seen fairly late in the season, while away beyond the ditch and racecourses is a private Cambridgeshire site for spiked speedwell, though I know this only from report and have not seen it myself. Clustered bellflower used to be found frequently on the chalk in our region (and it is also a plant in some areas of the dunes and even seacliffs), but is now scarce, and seems to have disappeared entirely from north-east Essex. I have seen a white-flowered form, but just outside our region on Therfield Heath in Hertfordshire.

The Ditch embankment bears the range of chalk-loving plants we have come to expect on ancient, unploughed chalk grassland. There is lots of sainfoin, *Onobrychis viciifolia*, in a fresh, bright pink which differs just enough from its neighbouring peaflower, the slightly darker, muddier rest-harrow. Sainfoin comes charmingly from the French for 'wholesome hay', and avid grazing of the plant allegedly induces cows to yield more milk, so by analogy sainfoin was recommended for nursing mothers. *Onobrychis* is Greek for 'braying ass', as some species were said to be a favourite food of that animal. The name rest-harrow, it seems, derives from the tendency of the matted roots to impede the old horse-drawn ploughs and harrows.

But what we really cross into Cambridgeshire to see earlier in the year, between late March and May, is one of the glories of the flora: the sumptuous purple and gold Pasque-flower, a native but very local anemone of dry, warm, south or south-west slopes of calcareous grassland. It is limited to a handful of sites in central and eastern England, from west Gloucestershire to Cambridgeshire and north Lincolnshire. Sadly, it has not been seen in the wild in Norfolk since the early 19th century, when it grew on the Tulip Hills near Lexham, which were probably named after its somewhat tulip-shaped blooms. Simpson pronounces it 'probably extinct' in Suffolk (which some might think errs on the side of caution) and remarks that formerly it was probably frequent around Bury St Edmunds. It was last seen on the linear earthwork crossing Cavenham Heath to Icklingham in the 18th century. It rarely if ever colonises new sites. The bell-shaped velvety flower, with prominent yellow anthers, is at first erect then later drooping, and is then replaced in fruit by long silky plumes. It is said to have been called the passeflower originally (the root, when boiled in raisin wine or 'passum' was thought to be good for the eyes), but Gerard, the famous herbalist, recorded it as 'Pasque' in his *Herbal* of 1597, because it first flowers about Passion Week (and continues from early April to about 20 May). It was also the source of a green dye used to colour Easter eggs. It should be mentioned, however, that the plant has long been associated firmly with Easter in its French, Dutch and German common names. It can irritate the skin of some people simply by their brushing a hand over it, but in homeopathic medicine the tincture has been used, it is claimed, to ease menstrual pains. The first element of its scientific name, *Pulsatilla vulgaris*, means 'trembling' – which the flowers, largely unprotected at first by any great leaf-growth, are indeed liable to be found doing if any slight breeze stirs. The Suffolk alternative common name, 'Dane's-blood', refers to a fancy also indulged far beyond that county's boundaries that it sprang up where blood had fallen, perhaps suggesting its long association with earthworks of a partly military significance. However, it seems it did not respond to enemies and invaders alone, for Saxon blood replaces Danish in some versions of the name. In Cambridgeshire, Pasque-flowers were Coventry bells or Dane's flowers, whereas Dane's-blood could also be applied to the clustered bellflower.

The subject of blood brings us to another rarity of the Devil's Ditch, the bloody cranesbill, which was often made respectable by the fastidious Victorians as 'blood-red cranesbill'. My northern childhood means my prejudiced eyes see this plant as oddly alien on south-eastern chalk and as belonging on the harder, greyer limestone pavements and cliffs of the north-west, where it is relatively frequent.

A strong candidate for the title of Britain's most extraordinary native plant is the bizarre lizard orchid. It is occasionally called the goat orchid because of its somewhat foul smell, which attracts flies and other insects. Its strange flowers, which mix pale grey-green with whitish and brownish hues and fine purplish streaks and spots, include a long, twisted lip with crimson spots, like a lizard's tail. This gradually uncoils from the bud like a spring taken from a clockwork watch. The sepals and petals form a hood, into which the 'lizard' seems to have shouldered its way. Not just its odd appearance and rarity make the lizard an exciting plant to find, but also its comings-and-goings: the advances and retreats in its British distribution pattern over a relatively short period of time; its unreliability as to flowering and reluctance to remain at many sites it occupies; and its vagrant's penchant for appearing, unpredictably and often as a single plant, in what seems to be a new site and district. It was extremely rare before 1900 and restricted to the south-east, but then advanced rapidly north and west up to about 1930, by which time it had reached Yorkshire and Devon. A retreat was then sounded and now its encampments seem to offer hope of permanent occupation only in Kent, Sussex and Cambridgeshire, though there are fairly recent records in Wiltshire, Hampshire, Oxfordshire and, as regards East Anglia, in east Norfolk and Suffolk. It was thought that drier years encourage the wider establishment of new plants from wind-borne seeds, and though this theory was dented by a failure of the lizard orchid to make a comeback in the late 1970s and the 1980s it is said to have tripled its numbers nationally in the 1990s.

The lizard orchid appeared in Norfolk at Haddiscoe as late as 1923 and, though it has been recorded in recent years only in east Norfolk, it formerly appeared briefly and unpredictably more widely in the county. The first Suffolk record, at Marlesford Hall, was much earlier, in 1812, and all the early 20th-century records were in some 10 parishes in the east of the county. Since the 1950s, it has been found near Brandon, on Lakenheath Warren, and just outside Lakenheath itself, which became the most northerly British site. There were 40 plants at Lakenheath by 1985, but only four plants remained by the beginning of the 1990s. Despite this diminution, the unpredictability of the 'Lizzie' gives every orchid aficionado the faint hope of stumbling on a plant in the region. It usually grows in Britain on calcareous sites of scrub, woodland margins, often tallish grass, or old sand dunes. Its unfarmed, chalky Cambridgeshire site is its best hope of a permanent foothold in the region now, though plants were dug up and stolen from here quite recently, despite wardening.

Churchyards and wayside verges, even if not on the chalk, can be colourful refuges for grassland plants, though it is true that the base-rich sites do tend to be the ones possessing the more interesting species. Where country churchards are not given repeated all-over, crew-cut mowings on the regrettably still-common view that bowling-green neatness is next to Godliness, you may be blessed with the sight of the best show in the parish of primroses, violets and bugle in the spring, and bright, bold ox-eye daisies, yellow lady's bedstraw or fleaweed (once indeed slept upon because it was sweet-smelling and slow to succumb to infestation by fleas), various vetches, smaller cranesbills, clovers, trefoils and medicks in the summer. There may even be pyramidal or other orchids. Of course, grass pathways and the area immediately surrounding the newer graves may need to be shorn frequently, but restricting mowing of any herb-rich areas to a regime not dissimilar to that of an old hay meadow – including raking up the 'hay' – will pay a long-term dividend in flower colour and scent far surpassing any satisfaction to be gained from cropping nature into a billiard table imitation. Many churches were built, centuries ago, on pasture- or meadowland. Our county wildlife trusts survey likely churchyards, suggest wildlife areas and advise on their management – and sometimes local groups assist in that management. One hopes that villagers everywhere might come to cherish and maintain their parish wildflowers so.

A plant often found in our churchyards, though also occurring on well-drained roadside verges and banks, perhaps deserves special mention. Meadow saxifrage, sometimes known with rare and commendable lack of chauvinism as fair-maids-of-France, is scattered and no more than locally common over the greater part for the country, but is, to use the language of the plant recorders, uniquely 'frequent to abundant' in south Norfolk and northern part of Suffolk. You may find it still in ancient pastures and meadows (it particularly likes the better-drained situation found atop old anthills), on railway banks, along open rides in woods, on cricket fields and even, in Suffolk, on peaty sand skirting a fen near Mildenhall. But even though it seems to resist spraying on farmland pretty well, we are perhaps better used to seeing it as a closer neighbour than that, in the churchyard and along the lane. The generic element of *Saxifraga granulata* means 'breakstone', or 'rock-breaker', but the precise significance of this name is disputed: some say it derives from the fact that other species of the genus live in rock crevices or on stone walls, and appear to break through from them or break them up; others say the name derives from the alleged efficacy of some species in clearing bladder and kidney stones. The 'granulated' specific name refers to the bulbils in the axils of the lower leaves, by means of which the plant over-winters, and these bulbils were the parts boiled in wine to cleanse the kidneys. Meadow saxifrage is now very rare in north-east Essex, being limited to two churchyard sites, though it grows also just outside our area of Essex in Waterhall Meadows, Danbury.

Vicarage lawns and grass tennis-courts rather than churchyards were once more likely to host populations of the diminutive autumn lady's-tresses orchid, especially where the turf was originally obtained from local pastures. Of all our lady's-tresses species the tight spiral of flowers of this orchid best resembles a woman's plaited or braided hair. Unfortunately, this charming plant is increasingly rare, though there may be hundreds of leafless, dainty greeny-white flower spikes where and when it does occur. The best-known Norfolk site is the private orchid lawn at Greshams School, where I have seen many dozens in flower, though it also grew at Beeston Regis, Caldecote Fen, Foulden and in the downland turf of the NWT Ringstead reserve. There was also the interesting Holt Country Park site, where the autumn lady's-tresses grew not far from creeping lady's-tresses before the former disappeared. The site of an old tennis-court at Theberton now seems to be Suffolk's sole remaining location and two garden-lawn sites remain at Frinton and Great Horkesley in north-east Essex. There is a conservation problem now that the orchid relies on mown domestic grassland, for it needs dry summers, when mowing stops or pauses before August, in order to flower and it may not survive decapitation for year upon year, despite its capacity to reproduce vegetatively.

We have a fair number of unusual clovers in the region, including one whose flower resembles a fruit, the strawberry clover; one that buries its head (its fruiting head, that is) in the ground, the burrowing clover; one whose leaves are like an animal's foot, the haresfoot clover; and one that seems to try to conceal and stifle its flowers amongst its calyx-teeth and leaves, the suffocated clover. But all these are distributed more widely than East Anglia, whereas the sulphur clover, *Trifolium ochroleucon*, is very much a long-lived perennial of our region, though it does manage to push thinly westwards as far as Northamptonshire. Though it is commonest just outside Breckland on the boulder clay of south-east Norfolk and similar deposits in Suffolk, it is like many of the special Brecklanders in being one of the 'continental' species with a foothold in Britain only in the area of lowest rainfall. It is a good unusual plant for hunting down, as you can spot it from a car owing to its fondness for shortish or sparse grass along roadside verges – sometimes right at the edge of the tarmac. Much less commonly, it grows along railway cuttings and banks and in lightly-grazed old pastures: the Suffolk Wildlife Trust Reserve at Winks Meadow, Metfield, is a good site. 'Sulphur' and *ochroleucon* describe the straw-colour of the flowerheads and, though it is often rather pale until some flowers turn brown with age like those of the white clover, in practice you can easily distinguish it from the commoner species once you have actually seen it.

The sulphur clover is very local and decreasing, and is threatened by road widening and realigning, by roadside public works such as cable-laying, and by the habit of mowing verges frequently, like garden lawns, near villages and along the frontages of houses and farms. Try the verges of the Wattisham and Semer areas in Suffolk, the area around Sapiston and east of North Lopham in Breckland, or south of Woodton in the Topcroft area of Norfolk. Recent survey work in north-east Essex revealed a dozen or so sites mainly at the edge of bridleways and grassy tracks towards the north-west of the area, south of Sudbury.

A useful short cut to sulphur clover is to consult the Suffolk Wildlife Trust's reserves handbook, *Watching Wildlife in Suffolk*, which lists roadside verge reserves carrying the plant and many other interesting roadsiders. It is good news that the Norfolk Trust, in cooperation with the County Council, has begun to establish wayside verge reserves in that county. A drive through Suffolk always had a touch of adventure for the wildflower aficionado, as one never knew when the familiar white posts marked 'NR' might appear at the roadside, necessitating a halt and a scrutinising of the verge in the hope it would yield its treasures in flower. The old-style posts remaining on about six sites were replaced in the spring of 1996 with new white posts bearing the SWT and Suffolk County Council logos and the words 'Roadside Nature Reserve'. Look out now also for Norfolk's new oak posts with small white plaques, and, for sulphur clover, visit the Bedingham – Topcroft roadside nature reserve described in the Trust Handbook.

East Anglian verges have suffered widely from cutting by flail mowers, which unfortunately leave their cuttings *in situ* to build up soil fertility, thereby encouraging the coarser, taller, quicker-growing plants such as hogweed, cow parsley and, where conditions are a little damper, great willowherb: all at the expense of more delicate, shorter and slower-growing wild flowers. Nor have the old green lanes of East Anglia survived unmolested as sites for such species as sulphur clover, for stretches of some are regularly appropriated for cross-country tracks by motorcyclists or play areas by drivers of faddish off-the-road vehicles, whilst others have even been ploughed. On the other hand, we have gained for the ox-eye daisies and the campions wide new verges and even more extensive grassy areas at the roundabouts and interchanges of motorways and new dual carriageways. Particularly interesting has been the tendency of flowers associated with the coast to make vehicle-assisted advances far inland along the central reservations and roadsides which are showered with salt spray and run-off in the wintertime: the white or pale lilac early scurvy-grass is the most noticeable of these. Where new verges are prepared with wildlife habitats in mind, such as along some chalky sections of the Thetford bypass, the wildflower interest of the district is enhanced. But where the new verges are covered with a layer of topsoil and seeded with often unsuitable species, rather than allowing recolonisation by wild plants, an 'artificial' verge, costly to maintain if maintainable at all, is created.

One always gets a 'buzz' from finding grassland orchids thriving on roadside verges. Though it cannot be described as common, the bee orchid is not as scarce as people seem to think, judging from their excitement and readiness to report it when they spot it on a wayside site. You have a sporting chance of coming across it also in quarries and pits, embankments, railway cuttings, older calcareous dunes, along sandy rides in pine plantations (and even under the trees at Strumpshaw in east Norfolk), and indeed, on any other surviving rough, chalky or even neutral grassland, though it does prefer the boulder clay. It has been known to colonise abandoned arable after a few years and has occupied former airfields – those at Parham, Ellough and Rattlesden in Suffolk, for instance, and at Hethel in Norfolk where it also grows on grassy verges in the private grounds of the Lotus Car Factory, despite mowing.

You might expect to be finding it daily, but a problem is its essentially monocarpic nature. Though plants may produce flower spikes for up to eight years or more, the great majority seem to flower only once, so it is an infuriatingly sporadic, fluctuating, uncertain species and a host of spikes one year may give way to one or two, or even none at all, the next. I know of one roadside site near Topcroft in south Norfolk where the bee orchid spikes once produced the illusion of decamping *en masse* and crossing the road from one verge to the other between flowering seasons!

The standard bee orchid flower has three pinkish sepals with green veins and two pale brown or greenish-brown sepals with rolled margins so they mimic a bee's antennae. The rounded lip completes the 'bee-on-a-pink-flower' effect with its base colour of velvety- or red-brown, with yellow-gold and deeper markings. But flowers are variable and bee orchid hunting is interesting: try the SWT roadside verge reserve at Great Blakenham for the variety *chlorantha* (seemingly the same as var. *flavescens*), a partial albino with a sage-green or yellow lip and whitish sepals. The so-called wasp orchid, var. *trollii*, which is a bee orchid with a long, pointed lip and brown, yellow and green markings, was discovered on a Cookley roadside verge after a period of 30 years during which no wasp orchids were found in Suffolk. There are even occasional white bee orchids: they are certainly present in Essex, but just south of our region at Asheldham Pits near Southminster. Even if you do not find these varieties, populations of bee orchids still sometimes yield various unsymmetrical 'peloric' mutants.

Although bees certainly do visit bee orchids – leaf-cutter bees, for instance, sometimes remove the lips for nesting material – fertilisation occurring as a result of attempts to copulate with the flower seems much more a feature of Mediterranean bee orchid fertilisation than of East Anglian plants, which are nearly always self-fertilised.

Another *ophrys* insect-mimicking species is the fly orchid, with its universally-admired dusky inflorescence featuring an iridescent blue or violet band across the middle of its long, triple-lobed reddish-brown lip, though no two observers concur in describing its colouring. The fly is now extremely rare in East Anglia and its two known Suffolk sites are, unsurprisingly, kept secret by those in the know. The fly orchid is not, like the bee, a plant of open grassland, but prefers woods, scrub, coppices and rough, grassy shaded habitats on calcareous soils. The plants are visited by male *Gorytes* wasps, but again attempts to copulate with the flowers have been observed in relation to continental plants, but rarely if at all when it comes to English fly orchids.

A widespread, fairly adaptable orchid that you may find in old broadleaved woods and occasionally secondary woodland, as well as open, grassy places including roadside verges, is the common spotted orchid. It does not, however, like the shade within the wood, but sometimes thrives in considerable numbers along grassy rides, hence its alternative name of wood spotted orchid. Though a generalist that can also be found in the drier parts of fens and marshes, dunes, commons, greens, railway cuttings, disused airfields, old chalk pits and clifftop sites, it does prefer calcareous soils. The lip is often mauve or pinkish, but can range through paler hues to almost white, with a fairly symmetrical double loop of broken lines and dots in darker mauve or purple. The closely-related heath spotted orchid – it was not distinguished as a separate species before this century – prefers acid to alkaline or neutral soils and shuns woodland. It can be locally abundant on moorland in the north and west of

Britain, and prefers heathy pastures and marshes in East Anglia. It can be found on a good many such sites in south-central and eastern Suffolk, but avoids the Breck. It is still findable in Norfolk but the 'improvement' of old acid grassland has undoubtedly reduced its numbers and it seems to have disappeared from north-east Essex since its Tiptree Heath site was vandalised. I think the most reliable way to distinguish the heath spotted from the common spotted is to look for the usual wide, often very slightly frilly-edged lip of the former, which always has a central lobe much smaller than the two outer – like a small, sharp tooth as often as not. In any case, the two species rarely grow side-by-side.

A pink orchid, without flower markings that is also quite frequently found on chalky, grassy, roadside verges is the pyramidal orchid. In fact, the majority of its Suffolk sites are now such verges, and it is often associated with sulphur clover in the parishes of the South Elmhams and Ilkestshals. Similar sites are quite plentiful across in south Norfolk in, for instance, the Topcroft/Denton/Alburgh district. To see it still in a meadowland setting, visit Winks Meadow at Metfield and Martin's and High House Meadows at Monewden. As for railway banks and cuttings, there are those at Hadleigh, Lavenham and Welnetham in Suffolk, and Narborough in Norfolk. These are relatively recent equivalents of such earlier man-made chalky grassland habitats as the Devil's Dyke in Cambridgeshire and the circular embankments of Warham Camp, near Wells in Norfolk, with its lovely curves of pyramidal orchids. A good dune site is the NWT Holme Dunes reserve and this enterprising orchid can also be found in open scrub and chalkpits and on banks, old airfields and rougher, unimproved grassland in general. It tolerates quite tall grasses such as are found in unmown churchyards and cemeteries, often growing tall and more willowy itself in such conditions. It is rare in Breckland. The pyramidal orchid is attractively tight and bright when it first opens from mid-June on into August, and its usually solid-pink flower spike, still unopen at the top, gives the pyramidal configuration from which its name derives. Later it becomes more rounded and domed. Its unspotted leaves are usually withered by this time. There can be pure white flowers, or they can range from pale pink to deep red. They have a modest but sweet scent, attracting butterflies and moths, especially burnet moths.

The rarest of our wayside orchids, now a Suffolk speciality (though there was a post-1970 record in a north-west Norfolk coastal tetrad), is the man, or green man orchid, with yellowish-green, sometimes brownish flowers which look like a dangling human figure. The hood often has a red-brown border and the 'arms and legs' are also sometimes reddish-brown, especially in very sunny situations. The scent is not pleasant, but attracts midges, ants and hover-flies. It is a plant of south-east England, from Lincolnshire southwards, and can be found on dry chalk or limestone slopes and on field boundaries, old chalk pastures, the sides of chalk pits and even amongst open scrub. In Suffolk, before a lawn site was recently reported, it seems the orchid grew in only four places (including three SWT protected verge sites): that is, Flowton, Wattisham, Nedging and Little Blakenham. Possibly, it lurks unnoticed on other verges: the man orchids on the Flowton verge came to light in 1968 when mowing was postponed to allow sulphur clover on the site to flower.

North-east Essex and neighbouring parts of Suffolk in the valley of the Stour and its tributaries are the British stronghold of another notable perennial – though a short-lived one – which is much rarer or absent elsewhere. This is the lesser calamint, quite easily confused in the field with the common calamint, which is actually much less common than the lesser in this area of Suffolk and probably totally absent from north-east Essex! In Norfolk, however, the lesser calamint is the rarer species, recorded in only four tetrads since 1970. The best route through these perplexities is again to find the Suffolk sites for lesser calamint in the SWT Reserves Handbook roadside verges section, and make for one of them in the confidence that there is a fair chance you will find yourself looking at the right plant. It likes dry, warm sites on light sandy or gravelly soils and is now largely a wayside plant of south-facing banks, though it sometimes grows in churchyards and, extraordinarily, on the north side of the Roman Wall at Colchester. It produces lots of seed, but plants can be killed by spells of intense winter cold and sites have also reduced because of the mowing of verges and churchyards.

It is seldom that a rare plant is also so large and conspicuous that it is difficult to miss it on the roadside verge as one drives by. Hoary mullein, despite growing up to four feet high or more, was not recognised as a distinct species until 1745 when someone examined a plant growing beside the old city wall of Norwich and noticed that the mealy white fluff that coats the plant grows on the stem and both sides of the leaves, distinguishing it from the great and the white mulleins. It is splendidly distinctive: some have compared it to a candelabrum, others to a yellow, white and dark-green christmas tree. East Anglia is its home ground in Britain (though it occurs casually in other regions) yet the shingle on the eastern side of the Wash is its only natural habitat here and it is perhaps commonest in north-west Norfolk. But it has other favourite haunts, especially Norwich and its outskirts, where you may find it on railway banks and cuttings, chalk and gravel pits, river banks and almost any waste or marginal land with some chalk. But it seems to like roadside verges above all in this area, where you may catch sight of just one of two plants, but where stately colonies soon build up by the roadside like groups of patient pedestrians waiting until they can cross in dignified ease. It is said to take two to four years to flower, but hoary mullein soon colonised the Cringleford bypass south of Norwich to such good effect that a plant or two appeared on the very narrow central reservation, as if stranded halfway across this busy stretch of the A11. It is also pleasing to see the species now stiffly observing from more than one vantage point the intemperate, headlong dash of traffic along the new Norwich southern bypass.

In Suffolk, the mullein is less commonly seen, though it can be locally abundant. It is largely restricted to two districts: the Beccles – Lowestoft area and the country around Bury St Edmunds. In north-east Essex, there are a few plants on a railway site at Colchester and at Parkeston. It has been recorded in 65 Norfolk and Suffolk tetrads since 1970.

Hoary mullein's close relative, great mullein or Aaron's-rod, was formerly known as the Candlemas-plant, lady's-candle, or torches, and the hag's-, king's-, or high-taper – partly because it resembles a candle, but also because the down of its leaves was used for tinder and wicks before cotton wicks for lamps came in. One imagines the hoary mullein would have given even better value in this respect. Aaron's rod was the flannel-flower in Suffolk and flannel-jacket in Norfolk. Extraordinarily, the seeds were once smoked with tobacco to relieve asthma, which seems rather like drinking alcohol to cure a hangover.

One never knows what may turn up on roadside verges, either inexplicably, or cast out as garden rubbish, or planted. Some of these 'escaped' or introduced garden flowers may thrive well enough, at least for a while, but seem ill-at-ease and out of place: many highly-bred daffodils, for instance, are much less effective on semi-wild verges outside houses and farms than the more restrained wild daffodil or Lent lily, which was once Queen Anne's flower in parts of Norfolk. In the west and north of England – in Wordsworth's Lake District, for instance – one finds the wild daffodil most often in not-too-dense woodland, or at least ground with some tree cover, but not necessarily so in East Anglia, where it is much less common as a native plant, though quite widely introduced. There is indeed a good display in Water Wood, Butley, Suffolk, but the plant is also found in our region in meadows and pastures and on the banks of streams. There are a number of other Suffolk sites, such as the woods on the Benacre National Nature Reserve, but it is very rare in remaining woods in north-east Essex. It is also rare as a truly wild plant in Norfolk, but 'Petch and Swann' stated in the 1960s that it was to be found in meadows at Hethel where it had been known for many years, and, indeed, you can still see a fine show in the churchyard there, though adulterated a little by plantings of garden daffodils. Even finer is the March display in the churchyard at nearby Stoke Holy Cross.

We may resent the destruction of old meadows, but when we see arable fields devoid of the old bright weeds of the corn, we merely sigh, for it would indeed be unreasonable and unrealistic to expect farmers to tolerate the adulteration of grain by, say, corncockle seeds (which Gerard's *Herbal* says makes bread objectionable in 'colour, taste and unholsomnes'), even if the price is the virtual extinction of this lovely purple flower in the wild. Its scientific name is *Agrostemma githago*, and for once the generic name is not just coldly appropriate: it means 'field garland'. It was known as the cockerel in parts of Suffolk, and the popple more widely in East Anglia.

Not that all our showiest arable weeds are native: the corncockle came from the eastern Mediterranean and the bright corn marigold is also an introduced species. I must admit the best show I have seen of the marigold was in a field of barley far north on Tayside, brilliant one evening beneath a purple-black Scottish sky because side-lit by sunbeams streaming from the only narrow cleft in the stormy cloud canopy. But the corn marigold is – or was – plentiful in East Anglia on the lighter soils and I have often seen good shows (though never a fieldful) on the acid sands just north of Norwich. The scientific name, *Chrysanthemum segetum*, means 'gold flower of cornfields' and in some moods the strong yellow of the marigold amongst the paler crop can be more pleasing than the blinding scarlet-and-straw contrast of poppies and corn. Anciently, it was known simply as gold and regarded as a pernicious arable weed, but its East Anglian local name was boodle, or sometimes buddle. The flowers are eaten in China.

We are also now denied the blue and gold of cornflowers in a wheat field. *Centaurea cyannus*, the cyan or dark-blue bluebottle, once also the pincushion in Suffolk, is now regarded by some as a native plant (though by others as an introduction from south-east Europe), but this does little to save it from demotion from a cornfield plant to an occasional garden-escape ignominiously condemned to waste places. This 'destroying beauty' of the corn has declined owing to the screening of seed and the use of chemical herbicides. Just very occasionally some deep ploughing or other disturbance of one of its old haunts (the widespread laying of gas pipes in recent years, for instance) releases locked-up seed to produce a show giving a pale reflection of former glories. Only one persistent British site remains now – in mid Suffolk. An infusion once made from the dried florets of cornflowers was used as an eye-bath for conjunctivitis, a mouthwash for bleeding gums, and for treating dropsy and constipation.

Sprays, seed-destroying stubble burning, improved seed-cleaning and other developments in farming methods have all driven the lilies from our cereal fields (which are, after all, grass monocultures), but it is an ill-wind that allows no weeds to blow more profusely. Though once-universal, colourful arable weeds such as charlock now seem to be much more rarely seen, a few others have taken grateful advantage of the reduced competition or have resisted sprays. And it has been pointed out that the more closely related a weed species is to the cereal crops in which it grows, the less likely it is to be bothered by the chemical controls that are formulated to spare that cereal crop. The recent 'set-aside' policy has also had interesting effects: some chalky ex-arable fields in Breckland were crammed in the summer of 1993 with the admittedly not-ravishing Canadian fleabane and I have seen one lapsed arable field on the boulder clay in South Norfolk solid with dandelions like certain alpine pastures and another bearing hundreds of spikes of common broomrape amongst the rejuvenated white clover. But land set aside unworked for a number of years will not allow sustained spectacular displays of the brighter opportunist weeds that depend on the soil being broken and disturbed annually.

A field of ripe wheat is a fine sight to the farmer, and I must admit also to being a less than wholehearted adherent to the fashionable view that rape-fields are to be despised – even if the bee-keepers do think they ruin the prospect of delicately-flavoured honey. Do we expect all pastel subtlety in high summer in an area that, for better or worse, is predominantly arable rather than pastoral? A blinding field of brassy rape set off by the cool, unmoved light blue of the ever-more-common linseed in an adjoining field has its place if we cannot have corn marigolds and cornflowers *en masse*. And I am told that the sprays used on rape do not affect poppies, so perhaps we may look forward to a battle of vibrant red and shrieking yellow, though I have only seen poppies on the margins of rape fields to date.

I have thus left until last the arable weed that most readily, and perhaps most fondly, springs to mind, for it flatters our hope that nature's resourcefulness, tenacity, and recuperative powers surpass our capacity to exhaust them. This flower is of course the common, corn, or field poppy – otherwise called the canker, canker rose or corn rose, or the red weed: all names used at different times and places in East Anglia (though canker weed was usually applied instead to ragwort in Suffolk). In other regions, variant names show an unqualified liking for the flowers – among them butterfly ladies, red dolly and red petticoat. The alternative local names for the poppy, and the number of them, well express what a curious mixture of friend and foe this vivid flower has been: its seeds can be sprinkled on bread, cake and biscuits and its dried petals used in pot pourris and herbal teas or employed to make a cough-soothing infusion, for instance; yet smelling the flowers was thought to bring on a headache (or to relieve one you already had), and another East Anglian name was, indeed, headache. There is an old superstition that gazing on poppies in the mass may cause blindness, so it was called blind-man, blind-eyes and blindy-buffs in other English regions, and even collected earaches as an additional local name in the North Midlands. Roy Vickery records a Cambridgeshire belief surviving into the 20th century that sniffing the flowers could cause nosebleeds, which should be cured by putting cobwebs up the nostrils! If you handled the plant excessively, then assuredly warts would result. It was thought in some places that picking poppies caused thunderstorms, so the plant acquired the names thunderflower, thunder-cup, thunderbolt and lightnings. Its most sinister local names were poison poppy and Devil's tongue. In Ireland, an old Gaelic name for the poppy was, in translation, red chaff, indicating its tendency to an obvious and undesirable presence in the threshing and winnowing of the wheat. Associating the Flanders poppy with the blood so copiously spilt on the World War I battlefields required only the extension and enrichment of an established symbol, for the poppy had old military connections in its Norfolk name of soldiers and, elsewhere, red soldiers. Its scientific generic name, *Papaver*, is from the Latin *pappa*, or milk, referring to the milky latex, and the English 'poppy' comes from the Anglo-Saxon *papig* of uncertain origin (though Geoffrey Grigson suggested a possible line to the ancient Sumerian *pa pa* through the Latin).

Though our memory insists the poppy once grew in greater numbers in more fields, it would be perverse to class it with the arable weeds under immediate threat of extinction, for almost every East Anglian has seen at least part of a field ablaze with poppies, or a bank beside a newly-made road scarlet in high summer. Indeed, a poppy-field is the exemplar from which most people now derive their idea of what an arable field dominated by a single species of wildflower is like. We may not realise that a field can contain hundreds of millions of poppy seeds, a fair proportion of which can lie dormant for 40 years or more, but we see advance guards and scouting parties of poppies whenever a roadside verge suffers a scrape, and we sense that the countless redcoats are lying low, ready to reoccupy territory when a spray is omitted, or fails to take, or misses a corner, or a building project creates the conditions for mass germination.

It is pleasant to dwell on the indomitable poppy and its obstinately viable seeds: Richard Mabey writes memorably that no one has yet found a collection of poppy seeds so old that none of them will germinate. But it is the exception to the rule that most kinds of lilies of the field are in enforced decline. The bleak truth is that future generations are likely to find it increasingly difficult to decide for themselves in the general countryside that Solomon in all his glory indeed could not have been arrayed as one of these. They will have to depend on scattered old grassland sites preserved by private eccentricity, public affection, or by conservation bodies, as reserves, but at least it is relatively easy to conserve old hay meadows through traditional mowing and grazing or equivalent modern regimes. The conservation of arable weeds is a knottier problem, though some farmers have been persuaded to follow the adage of leaving the field edge unsprayed to gain some partridges. We can take heart at the combined efforts of the conservation bodies, local volunteer groups, and school parties and the like who now do so much to maintain and, within limits, restore the flower-rich sites of East Anglia, but so much is now lost and irredeemable.

South Norfolk cowslips.

LEFT: Yellow rattle. RIGHT: Ox-eye daisies. BELOW: Suffolk buttercups in Winks Meadow, Metfield.

LEFT: Green-winged orchid. RIGHT: Frog orchid. BELOW: White, flecked and dark-coloured forms of the early-purple orchid.

LEFT: Rock-rose. RIGHT: Kidney vetch. BELOW: Squinancywort and thyme.

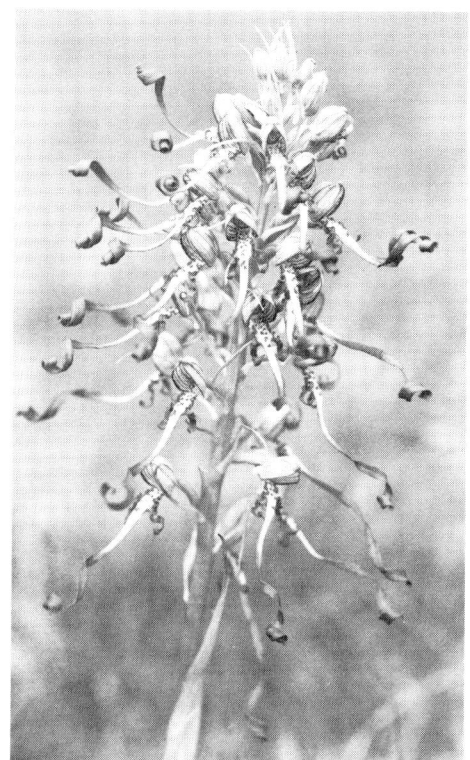

LEFT: Sainfoin. RIGHT: Lizard orchid. BELOW: Pasque-flower.

Meadow saxifrage and horse chestnut at Shotesham, Norfolk.

LEFT: Common spotted-orchid. CENTRE: Autumn lady's-tresses.
RIGHT: Man orchid.

Lesser calamint. INSET: Pyramidal orchid.

Spring renewal: wild daffodils at Hethel, Norfolk.

LEFT: Hoary mullein. RIGHT: Bee orchid. BELOW: Unusual yellow
form of common broomrape.

42

Wildflowers fringing fields of oilseed rape and linseed.

LEFT: Yellow star-of-Bethlehem. RIGHT: Bluebell.

THE FLOWERS OF THE FOREST

> ...violets dim,
> But sweeter than the lids of Juno's eyes
> Or Cytherea's breath; pale primroses,
> ...bold oxlips...
>
> William Shakespeare, *The Winter's Tale*

The tendency for plants of the woodland floor to start into early growth and enjoy a precocious, brief flowering before they are shrouded by the newly-unfurled leaves of the overarching trees can make them potent symbols of untimely human loss. 'The flowers of the forest are withered away,' says the poet. But usually the early vigour and vernal blossoming of these woodland species stirs us more than does the subsequent fading and secures for them a happier place in our affections as exemplifications of renewed life breaking through winter's crust. It is to the greenwood we go, before indeed it is heavily green again, for the first, gladdening floral displays of the season.

We do have our East Anglian forests, of course, though not the broadleaved nor the often-treeless, deer-country, medieval kinds, but rather the modern, mainly coniferous sort, comprising expanses of adjacent plantations. But the wildflower riches are held by the smaller, broadleaved woods; principally those of ancient lineage, though secondary woodland – woods, that is, on sites that were once something else – is also seen to have acquired sometimes a fairly interesting ground flora.

Two notions about broadleaved woods – one romantic and the other rather practical – seem now to have percolated through to public consciousness. First, there is the seductive but apparently well-founded idea that very old and intricate woods trace their ancestry, unbroken in its essentials, to the original wildwood that came to cover the country after the grip of the last glaciation began to loosen some 13,000 years ago. This primal woodland achieved a relative stability – but also considerable complexity and variety – during the period from the 7500 to 4500 BC, when climatic conditions much like today's became established. Such ancient woods will have evolved naturally since and will have been modified over the centuries by human management, but descendants of some of the original tree communities will remain. This is because a wood can regenerate vegetatively from the stumps and suckers that remain even if it is periodically clear-felled.

This brings us to the second feature of ancient woods now commonly appreciated: the fact that for centuries coppicing was widely practised. This entailed selected tree species (usually hazel, ash, or maple and often also oak, lime or hornbeam – though all native broadleaved species will in fact regenerate vegetatively) being cut down to a stool, thus allowing them to sprout multiple stems which were in turn harvested at regular intervals when they reached a useful thickness and length. There is evidence of some coppicing having been practised well before 3,000 BC and it was widespread in England as early as Roman times. The trees were often coppiced every four or five years in the Middle Ages, though cutting at 10 or 20 year intervals became the more usual custom from the 16th century. This practice, rather surprisingly, extended the life of individual trees considerably, so that some coppiced stools really are medieval survivals. Some trees were allowed to grow unchecked as 'standards' among the coppiced stools in rotations of at least 30 years to provide timber for building and furniture, though care had to be taken not to allow, for instance, too many standard oaks per acre, or they would shade and reduce the value of the underwood, which produced a yearly income. The coppiced underwood itself was used to make hurdles, fences, tools, faggots, thatching spares and broaches, bean poles, pea sticks and the like, and – not to be underestimated – to provide firewood and sometimes charcoal. A wood was thus, as well as a provider of raw materials, an energy source no less than was a 19th-century colliery or is a modern power station, albeit of more modest capacity. But it had the advantage of being miraculously self-renewing and unconsuming of resources other than labour, so long as it was managed well.

A broadleaved wood was also a source of food, providing nuts, berries and fungi for human consumption. Fallen acorns once served in some oakwoods for pannage – the custom of allowing swine to roam the woodland floor in autumn – though the omniverous pigs must have threatened regeneration and the practice seems to have died out in the late Middle Ages. Wood-pastures, that is, woods managed at some time for both trees and livestock (with, for example, enclosures *within* a wood sometimes fenced off for deer), were often pollarded rather than coppiced, whereby the branches were regularly lopped off at a height of three metres or so to preserve the trees from grazing animals but also to provide, as with coppicing, a useful timber supply. We have one of the country's finest ancient wood-pastures, with magnificent pollard oaks, in Suffolk's Staverton Park. However, one would not expect a ground flora rivalling those of coppiced ancient woodland to have developed in such conditions of grazing and trampling. Woods also sometimes provided sheltered grazing for other farm animals tethered in grassy glades and the wider rides, though it must be said that keeping grazing beasts out of coppiced woodland was much the more usual preoccupation of woodsmen.

What is most important, from our botanical point of view, is the fact that the endurance and paradoxical stability of evolving, managed, coppiced, ancient woods provided favourable conditions for the development and preservation of a rich, complex flora of the woodland floor: coppicing was a botanical boon in that the periodic opening up of the tree canopy provided cyclical 'niche opportunities' for the herbs beneath, and promoted great flowerings in the years immediately succeeding the coppicing.

It is in the period of the late 19th century and afterwards, and particularly since World War II, that our medieval woods have been most extensively grubbed up and destroyed, mainly to produce farmland, but also for their sites to be replanted with conifers as a 'more economic' crop. Ancient broadleaved woodland has reduced by 50% since 1945 in many parts of lowland England, though some places, including Essex, have fared a little better. According to recent calculations, Essex in fact retains about 2.4% of its ancient woodland, Suffolk 1.1%, but Norfolk only 0.5%. One must hope that the process is halted by the preservation of woods as reserves and even in some cases by their resurgence as viable economic units providing, in addition to resources applied to surviving traditional purposes and articles, such contemporary renewable products as wood chips for gardens, charcoal for barbecues and, particularly in East Anglia, faggots (brushwood bundles) to combat coastal and riverbank erosion and – as a foundation for rubble – to help reconstitute scoured out riverbeds. Paradoxically, some recent opinion suggests that the area of ancient woodland may now actually be increasing slightly because of the frequent failure of conifer plantings on ancient woodland sites owing to the unsuitability of the land and to the effects of neighbouring trees.

Such is the individuality of East Anglian woods that you never quite know, as a first-time visitor, what you will find, and the tree and herb species can never be predicted with certainty from Ordnance and Geological Survey Maps or even from one's own knowledge of nearby or adjoining woodland. Many ancient woods have, for instance, standard oaks in common, but the coppiced species differ: Coombs Wood near Stowmarket has hazel and ash coppice, whereas Bulls Wood near Lavenham has, additionally, coppiced field maple; Groton Wood near Sudbury has coppiced small-leaved lime where the standard oaks stood before 20th-century felling, and Wayland Wood near Watton, across in Norfolk, has large numbers of the sweet-blossomed bird cherry in with the coppiced hazel.

This uncertainty as to which species woods will contain, combined with their air of mystery (Oliver Rackham writes of mesolithic man having hunted beneath the limes and drunk from the mysterious pools one so often finds), gives our woods an allure unlike that possessed by any other habitat. And the cathedral-like hush and sense of time suspended in some woods on calm days belies the evidence all around of growth, decay and change. But on breezy days there are whisperings in the canopy and stirrings along the rides, and in out-and-out gales the treetops sway and clash exhilaratingly. Woods attract myth and legend, the best known instance in our region being the attribution of the Babes-in-the-Wood folk-tale to Wayland Wood. It is easy to prefer the fanciful, relatively modern misinterpretation of the name as 'Wailing Wood', reflecting the cries of the abandoned babes, to the 'Wanelund', derived from Old Norse *lundr* or 'sacred grove', that once it was. On the subject of the potency of woodland names, one wonders if even a modern child would relish the prospect of a walk alone through Suffolk's Wolves Wood.

Woods proclaim their own history not only through the ponds and pools but also through their possession of such features as animal-excluding boundary banks, now sometimes within the expanded woodland, which may mark the old division of a wood between sub-manors, farms or other entities, as at Bonny Wood (a more inviting name!) near Stowmarket and the Bradfield Woods, among many others. Sometimes a parish boundary cuts through a wood, and the mix of tree- and flower-species differs on either side, as in Foxley Wood near Bawdeswell in Norfolk. And the relics of man's intervention can be more recent: coniferisation (including larches at Foxley), is an unwelcome sign of 19th-century planting in ancient woodland in Suffolk's Reydon Wood and Norfolk's Thursford Wood; sycamores, recently felled, were planted in Lower Wood, Ashwellthorpe in the 1970s; concrete bunkers used for wartime ammunition storage for the former adjacent airfield survive as semi-overgrown mounds and ruins in the delightfully-named Honeypot Wood near Wendling, and concreted rides of the same vintage make a walk through Honeypot as easy as a pavement stroll.

The woodland flowers add to all this diversity. The density of tree-cover determines what can grow at any one time – or, at least, grow well and flower profusely – beneath. Enchanter's nightshade and dog's mercury, for instance, can grow in only 2% or so of the light reaching ground level outside the wood, and the rarer broad-leaved and violet helleborines push them close in the dim-habitat stakes. One needs a rock-steady tripod and a relatively calm day even in the most sheltered recesses to take passable, if interminably-exposed photographs of such species if one dislikes flash.

Vegetative reproduction – sometimes by runners – rather than seed is common in a shady environment where light, nutrients and soil water are limited, and woods often contain patches of a single species derived from the same original wildflower parent. Because vegetative reproduction is much more reliable than reproduction by seed in the intense competition on the woodland floor, clones containing daughters or 'ramets' tend to achieve dominance in a particular location, hence the formation of patches. The bluebell, wood anemone, ramsons, dog's mercury and yellow archangel are examples of such species likely to form patches within the wood. Indicator wildflowers species of ancient primary woodland, however, do not colonise across open ground, though occasionally they will spread into adjoining secondary woodland. Other plants found in old woodland that are basically grassland species, such as bugle and stitchwort, are less tolerant of shade, will usually prefer the rides, and will regenerate well from buried seed.

On the other hand, woodland plant species can also be found in intimate mixtures in ancient woodland – for instance, in the coppice of Norfolk's Swanton Great Wood – rather than exclusive expanses (though varied mixtures rarely occur in secondary woodland). When the amateur botanist, on surveying the flowers of old woods, finds himself puzzled by these intriguing instances of homogeneity here, heterogeneity there, he also finds he is contemplating an area of active and continuing woodland research in East Anglia (and no doubt beyond), as ecologists attempt to formulate and fathom the basis and intricacies of the 'Assembly Rules' that govern these matters. Long periods of observation and measurement may be required in long-established, relatively stable areas of woodland to yield meaningful results, so we must wait patiently to see what explanations emerge.

In 1943, a pupil of Griston School in Norfolk appeared with a picked bloom comprising a cluster of seven small yellow flowers, with a green band on the back of each of the six tepals, and thus prompted an unsuccessful eight-year woodland search by a local botanist for the site of this rarity. But in 1951 another schoolchild, 11-year-old James Potts of Watton Area School, found and picked another bloom and two small areas where the flower grew were at last pinpointed in Wayland Wood. This plant, the yellow star of Bethlehem, is a notoriously erratic flowerer and its leaves, though much smaller and possessing slight three-edged ridges, may be mistaken for those of the bluebell where the latter grows in numbers. The failure to locate the species previously in a wood with a good and varied ground flora, including bluebells, is therefore not surprising. However, there are grounds for suspecting *Gagea lutea* to be an introduction to Wayland, as it grows in a part of the wood less ancient than the main wood and outside the Great Woodbank, on land that may have been used at times for other purposes, such as grazing and even arable. The plants produced up to 60 flowers in 1951, which of course aided in its rediscovery. But in most seasons since they have produced many fewer blooms or have not flowered at all. The density of the tree canopy may be crucial here. The wood was sold to the Norfolk Wildlife Trust by Lord Walsingham in 1975, and I recall being taken to see the yellow star of Bethlehem by the warden at the end of the 1980s. There were a few flowers in two patches, though I was told that vandals dug up and stole a number a year or two later. A visit in the chilly early spring of 1996, however, revealed six plants bravely flowering in the patch I found. It seems imperative in such circumstances not to indicate in which quarter of Wayland this shy but modestly appealing little bulbous perennial grows. It flowers in March and April, and searching for it when the distracting yellow of the lesser celandine studs extensive areas of the woodland floor is not calculated to leave one's patience untested.

Wayland is the only Norfolk site of the yellow star of Bethlehem, though it did grow at Castle Rising in the 19th century. It is very rare and decreasing in Suffolk and flowers regularly only at Great Glenham and Saxmundham, though it has been located in three

Suffolk hectads since 1970, and non- or rarely-flowering plants may lurk elsewhere, undiscovered even today. The species was thought to be scarce elsewhere in Britain and scattered thinly in even its heartland in northern England, but systematic searching in recent years has brought to light the existence of many new colonies so that, nationally, the yellow star of Bethlehem does not quite rank as a scarce species.

The genus *Gagea* has another East Anglian connection in that its name is taken from the Suffolk botanist, Sir Thomas Gage (1761-1820), whose grandfather had previously given the family surname to the greengage.

Better known and loved, and warmly welcomed in late winter – and more commonly found in our woods and hedgerows – is the snowdrop, yet the botanists tell us it is only 'possibly native', and achieves that equivocal status in south-western England, but not East Anglia, where it is introduced and long naturalised. There is no trace of the snowdrop in prehistoric pollen deposits and no record of it in the wild until the later 18th century. You do not even find its common name in use until the first half of the 17th century: improbably late for a familiar native plant. There is a suggestion that its name does not mean a 'drop' of snow (although snow falls in flakes, the name 'snowflake' is unavailable because spoken for by another genus of the daffodil family; nor is the unopened, nodding flower supposed to suggest the 'dropping' of a bead of fallen, accumulated snow, but rather, it is said, the drops resemble a snow-white version of ladies' pendants of the 16th and 17th centuries. Maybe, but our instincts are to resist an explanation which does not associate the plant as intimately as can be with the snow through which it so often bravely shoulders its way. You cannot get much more white and snowy than *Galanthus nivalis*, as *Galanthus* comes from Greek words meaning 'milk flower' and *nivalis* means 'of the snow'. Snowdrops have a sweet but restrained scent that attracts early hive-bees on sunny days, even in February.

You would rightly expect this bright, unsullied, early-flowerer to symbolise hope and purity (snowdrops were once fair maids in Norfolk), but there are also more wintry significations. A single snowdrop is a death-token, as the flower is – very fancifully – like a corpse in its shroud and, as is the case with nodding, head-hanging flowers in general, it is unlucky in the house. It is a wonder it gets anywhere near farms, as it supposedly makes the milk thin and the butter colourless of any cow that manages to graze it, and, for good measure, stops eggs hatching. It also stops intended marriages coming off as planned if you are astoundingly silly enough to pick it before Valentine's Day. A surviving Cambridgeshire belief has it that snowdrops outside the window bring happiness, but induce a parting if brought indoors.

The snowdrop's acquisition of this rich collection of positive and negative attributes perhaps sways the argument back in favour of its being long-established or even native in some regions; on the other hand it may merely indicate its strong impact on us in a relatively short career as garden-plant and escape.

In the 1960s, the snowdrop was described as being locally abundant in Norfolk, in damp woods and hedgebanks. In Suffolk, it is frequent as a naturalised plant of woods, copses, orchards, churchyards, hedgebanks and former gardens. My impression from my own home patch south of Norwich is that it is not in retreat and is in fact probably increasing from deliberate plantings near houses as well as from spreading along road banks from churchyards and garden throw-outs. The increase in gardening activity and in stocking gardens more richly in the last 20 or 30 years has given the snowdrop bases from which to advance or be loosed into the wild. Several garden cultivars have been developed from snowdrops of Norfolk origin. Certainly, they often endure and multiply on the sites of old gardens: I know several where snowdrop copses have now developed, and one where a large, old, semi-wild water garden with mature native trees, after draining and abandonment a half-century ago, became packed with a carpet of countless thousands of snowdrops interrupted only by a band of brilliant yellow winter aconites, for all the world as if they had always been there in such dazzling numbers.

If one pictures a broadleaved wood in spring, the ground flowers that come to mind are not especially characteristic of East Anglia, but might add to the 'gladness of the time' almost anywhere in England. One thinks of carpets of wood anemones. One thinks of more scattered, fresh, light-yellow primroses setting off dim violets. Early-purple orchids – a little later into flower, but the spikes up and the still-tight florets beginning to acquire colour – are also there.

Dog violets, as the name suggests, are the commonest and most taken for granted (they have been called horse violets in Essex), but are lovely to see nonetheless. They are flowering happily by March: indeed, the bluish-mauve early dog-violet can flower in early February in a favoured season and spot. The more often found blue-violet flowers of the common dog-violet first come a mite later, though there is a considerable overlap. Floras seem always to assume that violets present no real identification problems to the novice, but my experience is that they vary somewhat within each species, and though the early dog possibly prefers dryish, more open sites, the two species are often near neighbours, and there seem sometimes to be hybrids to augment the amateur botanist's uncertainty. If you are lucky enough to find the less common sweet violet in a wood or hedgerow, identification is easier because of the famous evocative scent, even if the flowers can range from the typical violet colour to whites and, very rarely, pinks or apricots. Sweet violets are used for perfume, for love charms, to decorate food dishes such as fruit salads and ice cream, to flavour sweetmeats and rice puddings, as crystallised sweets and to treat catarrh and wounds. Like snowdrops and primroses they are unlucky in small numbers, but allegedly have the surpassing virtue of preventing drunkenness if worn, daisy-chain fashion, in a wreath round the neck. I have not heard that they repel vampires: try wild garlic instead.

Primroses are a universal favourite, despite some uncheering attributes: a 19th-century dearth of the plants in Cockfield, Suffolk, was associated by the villagers with a much earlier human depopulation owing to the plague. There is a quaint superstition in East Norfolk that if you bring 13 primrose flowers into the house as the first bunch of the season, then your hens and geese will hatch that season either 13 eggs only, or only one egg in 13.

If you happen to live on the higher parts of the chalky boulder clay near where south-west Suffolk, north-west Essex and south-east Cambridgeshire meet, your local ancient wood may contain another, nationally rare primula which some would argue outshines both primrose and cowslip in delicacy and grace. The true oxlip, *Primula elatior* (the specific name means it is the 'taller' primula), grows in Britain only in this area, apart from two small outlying areas in Buckinghamshire and another outlier at Dickleburgh Pightle in Norfolk where, however, it is reported as having been hybridised out of existence. Confusingly, it is sometimes called the paigle in Suffolk, which name one usually applies to the cowslip. It is also known as five-fingers, though this is also applied to the false oxlip here and there in East Anglia! It is often stated categorically that the true oxlip grows – often abundantly – only in woods on chalky boulder clay (which more or less lack the primrose), but Simpson has found small numbers in alder and willow carrs and swamps, along the borders of streams and rivers and even in old, wet pastures in Suffolk. Of course, woods could have stood formerly on some of these sites, yet it is curious that the British plant is found under tree-cover on the whole when its continental counterpart grows lustily in the open in western Europe, sometimes carpeting alpine pastures.

Until the 1840s, the name 'oxlip' was applied to crosses of the cowslip and the primrose, the name having developed analogously to 'cowslip' from old English *oxenslyppe*, meaning ox's slime, or oxpat. The determining of *Primula elatior* as a true, distinct species in Britain meant that the primrose-cowslip hybrid had to be re-christened the false oxlip (or ladies' fingers, though this local name is also sometimes applied to the bird's-eye trefoil and the kidney vetch). It is not too difficult to tell the true from the false: the true oxlip flower has rounded, not streaked, orange eyes, and its leaves are constricted abruptly like cowslips; the false oxlip, on the other hand, has flowers with starry yellow centres and streaks running up the petals, and has primrose-like leaves. Perhaps the easiest, most quickly-spotted difference is the fact that the upward 'spray' of flowers – the umbel on a scape – of the true oxlip nods rather elegantly to one side of the plant, while the flowers of the false oxlip splay out and usually hang randomly on all sides. It must be admitted, however, that where the oxlip, cowslip and primrose are concerned, all the crosses possible between any two and between all three species have been recorded in East Anglia. The flowers of the true oxlip are mainly of a pale primrose yellow, but delicately smaller than those of the primrose. The scent, suggestive of apricots, is also delicate. It flowers in April to May. There survives an old East Anglian belief that the oxlip has been in decline since the demise of the wild boar, as it allegedly depended on the droppings of this creature. Any very recent apparent decline may arise from the fact that deer eat oxlips and have increased in many old woods.

If you visit the Bradfield Woods in Suffolk to see the oxlips, you will notice along the rides good quantities of the wood spurge, a tall, downy plant with yellow-green cup flowers in a candelabra head. It is evergreen, but very susceptible to damage from late-spring frosts. 'Spurge' refers to the powerful purgative properties of most of the genus, and the acrid milky juices of spurges were used on warts. As well as damp woodland, wood spurge may be found in hedgebanks and the verges of former woodland: in north-east Essex it is reported as having adapted to ditchsides formerly close to such woodland. It is quite often met with throughout the region and there is a particularly thriving Norfolk population in Lower Wood, Ashwellthorpe. A further NWT reserve in which it occurs is Foxley Wood.

One thinks always of the wood anemone as being stirred by March gales or spring breezes even deep within old woods, but I suspect this is mainly owing to the fact that anemones are 'windflowers': a kind of red herring, as the name derives from *Anemone coronaria*, which is said to open in the wind but which is not found in the wild within hundreds of miles of Britain. Nonetheless, though our *Anemone nemorosa* is at its bounteous best in the 'well wooded' situations the specific name suggests, it is also found in hedgerows (often persisting when the hedge has gone), along wide woodland rides (in Norfolk's Swanton Great Wood, for instance), and even in open grassland in wetter districts of the country. Even in comparatively dry East Anglia there is an ebullient, large patch in the Suffolk Wildlife Trust's Mickfield Meadow (which was scrubby for a time). On my last visit, the anemone flowers here, with a few cowslips incongruously intermixed, seemed a little larger and more robust than most woodland wood anemones. Those in woods may be less obvious and floriferous later in the coppicing cycle as the canopy extends and thickens. The typical, solitary flower is white above its whorl of three leaf-like bracts, but colour variants add interest in some woods, as the flowers can also be variously tinged with purple, pink, mauve or – rarely – pale blue. There are quite deep reddish-purple variants in Wayland and Hockering Woods in Norfolk. Windflowers are reported to be still plentiful in north-east Essex, with little apparent loss over the last two decades. The classic site here is Stour Wood, where a range of flower colour-shades and petal-numbers (from five to 10) may be seen. Wood anemones are said to be poisonous to grazing animals, but pheasants like the flowers, which must inconvenience the fairies that, tradition insists, dwell beneath.

In concentrating on early flowerers found at their most plentiful in old woods on the boulder clay, I have missed a couple of little plants that thrive in rather different conditions, but which are irresistible in their restrained way. The first is the moschatel, so called because of its musky fragrance, like elder blossom, in damp weather, and flowering as early as March. It often grows in woods on light sandy or alluvial soils which yet are damp and have some humus present: you often see it pushing up through leaf-litter, for instance. Simpson reports it from alder-carr and valley woods in Suffolk and I have certainly seen it in similar places in Norfolk. Oddly, it also grows in shady, rocky places in mountainous parts of the country. Its flowers are modestly green (*Adoxa*, its scientific generic, means 'without glory'), but are good for getting children intrigued: another name for the plant is town-hall clock, because four flowers facing sideways look out at right-angles to each other: north, south, east and west, as it were. The additional upward-facing flower on top explains the alternative common name of five-faced bishop. It is not rare, but you do not see it in every wood. If you go to look for it too late in Copperas Wood, near the Stour in north-east Essex, you may have the consolation of seeing instead the common cow-wheat, increasingly rare in East Anglia.

The second plant is the dainty wood-sorrel, *Oxalis acetosella,* a low creeping perennial with white (or sometimes slightly purplish) flowers delightfully veined with mauve, that is also found in the mountains in highland Britain. In our region it is not fond of heavy clay, and it is also rare in the Breck. It haunts old woods, copses, lanes and streamsides and is often found growing in leaf litter, between twigs and branches or between the toes of large trees with roots visible at the surface. The three parts of the leaves often fold up curiously but attractively together and the plant may be the true St Patrick's shamrock. Some books recommend it as a salad vegetable and it has been grown in kitchen gardens, but beware: 'sorrel' derives ultimately from Low German *suur* (sour), *oxys* is Greek for acid (it contains oxalic acid), and *acetosella* is from the Latin *acetum,* also meaning sour! Though it has been used to sharpen sauces, it is said to be harmful in quantity, though children have traditionally nibbled it as a substitute for more substantial fare – hence its local names of bread-and-cheese plant, or egg-and-cheese. It tastes like a rather effete lemon to me, but is supposed to be reminiscent of true sorrel and Richard Mabey describes it as tasting of grape skins and reveals that American Indians fed its roots to their horses to make them gallop faster!

May, with its bluebells, is perhaps the time we regard our woods as attaining their greatest splendour, for many other attractive species are also in flower about then. We can be shamelessly chauvinistic about our bluebell woods and assert there is nothing elsewhere to match them. Certainly, there are bluebells in continental Europe, and woods in western maritime France and countries immediately to the north make what is, to the British eye, a half-hearted effort to rival them, but our packed oak or beechwoods, coolly blue with unending sappy richness, defy emulation. Even where the bluebell cover is not continuous, wide patches can seem to hang low above the woodland floor, like blue smoke with hyacinthine fragrance, or such a morning mist as never was. And nothing seems to clash with them: other flowers amongst or alongside bluebells are invariably set off to better effect.

Considering they are plants claimed as our own, we have been remiss in allowing bluebells to be bundled from genus to genus. They now seem to have settled as *Hyacinthoides non-scripta*, but they have sometimes been classified as *Scilla non-scriptus* and – my own favourite banished variant – *Endymion non-scriptus*. They *are* hyacinth-like, but what about *non scripta*? This means 'without marking' or 'unmarked'. It could signify that certain early hyacinths, in contrast, had marks on their petals or even that the plant was overlooked, or 'not marked' by the Greeks and Romans, but neither explanation convinces. It has been suggested that our bluebell is a hyacinth not marked with the 'letters of grief' that were evident on those plants that sprang, in Greek myth, from the blood of Hyacinthus. However, our bluebell does have a link with sorrow in that it shares with the grape hyacinth a reputation for inducing depression in the occupants if brought indoors.

Pentecostal bells – an alternative local name – are found in old woods, copses and ancient hedges throughout our region, often on lighter soils, though they avoid Breckland more assiduously even than the heavy clays, where they tend to keep to well-drained slopes, shady banks and wood margins. In wet areas of Britain (especially in Scotland, though the 'bluebell of Scotland' is always claimed to be the harebell), they grow also in grassland, but bluebells in East Anglia growing out in the open on banks or the like very often are relics of cleared ancient woods or hedges. There are occasional white, pink and purple flowered plants, provided they have escaped being stolen for gardens. The profuse, sticky sap in the stem was widely used in the Middle Ages to make a gum, one use of which was the gluing of the feathers or flights to arrow-shafts. In Elizabethan times, the sap was used to make a starch to stiffen ruffs.

It is difficult to be too angry with children who cannot resist picking a bunch from such plenty, and, indeed, the trampling accompanying such picking actually poses the greater threat to bluebell numbers. However, the grubbing up of a bluebell wood or copse for agricultural or building purposes, or the lifting of bulbs *en masse* by adults who should know better, is quite another matter. All bluebell woods should be cherished as if they were individual rare flowers. Together they form one of the brightest jewels in the crown of Britain's natural heritage, any facet of which cannot be dulled without dimming the glory of the whole.

A much more potent, and rather less gratifying odour overwhelms the scent of bluebells in woods which also contain ramsons, sometimes called ramsden in Norfolk, and otherwise known as wild or wood garlic. The common name in fact derives from the Old English *hramsa*, or rank, implying a strong smell and taste. The plant, indeed, is said to draw moles from the ground! As for the scientific name, *Allium ursinum*, the generic is from the Greek for garlic (though some suggest it derives from the Celtic word *all*, hot) and *ursinum* means 'pertaining to bears': perhaps they were fond of it or, more likely, it simply means a 'strong' or 'coarse' commonplace garlic on the model of the rather disparaging *horse*radish, but the leaves, in small quantity, have a milder taste than the smell of the plants in the mass would suggest. They can be used as a spring onion substitute in salads, and it is best to use the plant in salad form for medicinal applications: it reduces blood pressure very slightly and has been used to treat hypertension. The bruised leaves have been applied externally to abscesses and boils. But the plant allegedly produces unpleasant-tasting milk and butter if eaten by dairy cows.

ABOVE: Lily-of-the-valley among a host of its rare relation, the May lily, Swanton Great Wood, Norfolk. RIGHT: True oxlip, Felsham Hall Wood, Suffolk. BELOW: Spring flowers and lingering autumn leaves: dog violet and primrose in Wayland Wood, Norfolk.

Wild garlic grows on the banks of streams and rivers and in any shady, damp place as well as actual wet woods, usually on clay. In fact, great white stretches of it in old woods often give way quite abruptly to sheets of bluebells where the ground is suddenly just that little drier. There is a particularly good instance in a bluebell wood with public access on the National Trust Blickling Estate in Norfolk, where bluebells surround a pool of ramsons confined to a round, damp hollow.

Other woodland plants often associated with bluebells are stitchwort, red campion and yellow archangel, though I have seen the campion monopolising the ground flora in a secondary-woodland copse near Buxton in Norfolk. The common and infinitely less imposing red dead-nettle, related to yellow archangel, was once called red archangel in parts of Norfolk. Yellow archangel is pleasing so long as even its less vigorous variegated garden form does not run everywhere in your borders. It can be rampant also in the wild on clay soils, but its erect stems, up to 60cm high and bearing pale gold, hooded blossoms, are lovely rising among or just beyond the drooping bluebells, again where conditions become a little damper. The yellow is flecked with reddish honey-guides to direct the bees' attentions. It likes coppiced oak and ash woods, but Tarpey and Heath remark its yen in north-east Essex for damp conditions caused by seepage, including roadsides where there is copious run-off to keep the soil moist, and I have seen it on ditchsides far now from woodland. Weasel-snout rejoices in the scientific name of *Lamiastrum glaeobdolon* (or it may be either *Lamium galeobdolon* or *Galeobdolon luteum* in older floras). *Galeobdolon* means 'weasel stench', which libels the plant. Most woodland plants survive winter and prepare for early regrowth by means of storing food in underground bulbs, corms or rhizomes, but yellow archangel, like sanicle and bugle, develops new, though much less developed and numerous winter leaves to see it through.

Woodruff, or, even more charmingly, sweet woodruff, also likes damp, base-rich woods and hedgerows, but seems to have decreased somewhat since it was described as locally frequent in Norfolk in 1968. In Suffolk it was simply 'local' (in some 21 parishes) by 1982, and the 1990 north-east Essex flora recorded only five sites, but recalled the fact that the species was much more widespread in the late 19th century. The Anglo-Saxon name was *wude-rofe* or *wudurofe*, the *rofe* element in turn allegedly deriving from the French, *roue*, a wheel, probably because of the spoke-like arrangement of the leaves on the stem, though Geoffrey Grigson wondered if it meant the woodruff 'roves' or spreads in the wood. The sweetness of the plant – its new-mown-hay fragrance – explains the specific element of *Galium odoratum*, and it was in fact once hung in churches, strewn on floors and used to freshen linen by placing it in storage cupboards. The dried flowers are said to make a delicious tea and, as a fresh herb, woodruff has been used to flavour liqueurs, especially May-cups. *Galium* comes from the Greek for milk (as in *Galanthus*, the snowdrops), but refers not to the white flowers of woodruff, but to the fact that another member of the genus, lady's bedstraw, was once used to curdle milk.

There is a fair quantity of woodruff along the now-narrow central ride of the private Horningtoft Wood in Norfolk, as there is of a rather interesting hybrid that is sometimes found in damper woods. Herb-bennet or wood avens, with small, yellow, buttercup-like flowers, is a common woodland species. The dried plant has been used to make a medicinal tea for diarrhoea, upset stomach, or a sore throat, and has been applied externally to wounds. The dried root repels moths. It is the 'blessed herb' which drains potency from the Devil and drives him from your door. Its close relation, water avens, is a more attractive plant with nodding creamy-pink to purplish-pink blooms and it grows not only in marshes, fens, wet meadows and streamsides in our region, but also in damp woodland on the chalky boulder clay. It occurs frequently in Norfolk and West Suffolk, though no site was found in a recent survey in north-east Essex. Sometimes vigorous and fertile hybrids of these two Geums arise in wet woodlands, often producing flowers like those of water avens, but in a range of lovely, glowing colours covering a complete spectrum between the parents. Simpson mentions pure orange flowers in Suffolk and I have seen luminous shades from yellow towards orange in Norfolk. The hybrid has no English name and is generally referred to as *Geum X Intermedium*.

Herb paris is a scarce plant that does not possess conspicuous flowers but is nevertheless fascinating to those who penetrate deeply enough into our ancient woods to discover it. Because it shuns the edges of the damp, calcareous woods it prefers, and does not proclaim its existence by means of bright flowers, it is taken to be a little rarer than in fact it is. In Norfolk it prefers, though does not entirely limit itself to, the old woods on the central clay of the county. It can lay claim to being more plentifully distributed in Suffolk than perhaps any other county in England: Simpson remarks it has been found in the majority of primary woods and copses on the boulder clay and even turns up in secondary woodland adjacent to boulder clay. It is rare in north-east Essex, but may still be seen in Broadfield and Chalkney Woods.

Unfortunately, 'paris' implies no romantic French connection nor association with Trojan princes. Rather, it is simply from the Latin *par*, or equal, referring to the regularity of the plant's flower parts. It is the 'herb of equality' or 'pair herb' with, typically, two times two leaves, stamens, outer and inner perianth segments, styles and cells to the ovary. The specific element of its scientific name, *Paris quadrifolia*, also of course refers to its tendency to have four leaves and it is a curiously satisfying plant because of its symmetry, despite the leaves being so much larger than the tiny yellowish-green petals, and despite the foetid scent exuded to attract flies and, apparently, night-flying gnats. It is sometimes also known as 'one-berry' because of the single purple-black fruit it produces – but, inevitably, even this is cleft into four parts. However, it must be admitted that the number of leaves can vary from three to eight: I noticed what seemed to me a remarkable number of such variants recently in an arboreal rectangle not a mile from my home south of Norwich, which had formerly been old woodland but had been partly grubbed up and replanted with poplars and other standards at some time. A sufficient number of the old hazels and other coppiced trees had remained to require re-coppicing after a lengthy period and this often induces mutations in the shape of vigorous plants with 'extra' leaves. Herb paris is a powerful plant in folk medicine, efficacious, we are assured, against the effects of witchcraft, plague and poison, though it is in fact itself poisonous, but not deadly.

Also capable of growing in the darker recesses of ancient broadleaved woods are a number of orchids. We are used to thinking of orchids as showy plants and as the most glamorous and admired, if not necessarily the best-loved, members of our flora. Only orchids come close to being 'twitched' like the rarer wild birds and a drawing or photograph of an orchid presents the only flower that can rival badgers, otters, red squirrels and birds of prey as an appealing logo to represent a wildlife organisation, or as a potent emotive inducement to reach for the cheque book and contribute to a conservation appeal. Yet some of our woodland orchids are anything but showy. One such, the highly-specialised bird's-nest orchid, can grow in the darkest parts of woods because it has little chlorophyll and relies on the mycorrhizal fungi in its roots to pre-manufacture its food from the humusey soil beneath the rotting leaf-litter in which it usually grows. This saprophytic orchid has yellowish-brown or honey-coloured flower spikes which may seem dead from a distance, and, indeed, often rise alongside withered spikes persisting from the previous year. Very occasionally, there are sulphur-coloured or whitish flowers. Some say they smell sickly, some honey-sweet: I incline to the latter persuasion. They are hard to find in the arboreal gloom, and are rare in East Anglia now in woods and copses on humus-rich, calcareous, often clayey soils. The Suffolk Orchid Survey turned up some dozen sites, and a preference for mature coppice, often hazel, with low light levels seemed to be indicated, though elm scrub in an old railway cutting at Raydon also contained the orchid. This site is not to be confused with the SWT reserve of Reydon Wood, not far from Southwold, where the bird's-nest orchid also may be seen. It has been found in time past in Norfolk at Horningtoft, Hethel and Holt Country Park, and I have seen it in the NWT Ashwellthorpe Lower Wood. It has been lost, it seems, from its one remaining recorded site in north-east Essex.

But why bird's-nest? This name comes from the resemblance of the fleshy, tangled ball of roots to a bird's nest. The orchid certainly insists on the comparison in its scientific name, *Neottia nidus-avis*, for *Neottia* is from the Greek for bird's nest and *nidus-avis* is the same thing in Latin.

The twayblade is also an unshowy plant, though it does not grow only in damp woodland, but is one of our most adaptable orchids which may also be found on grassy slopes and in the drier parts of marshes, fens and wet meadows. It can colonise conifer plantations and chalkpits, and is one of the commonest European orchids, creating large colonies in some old woods, though it is reported to be much reduced in north-east Essex, and plentiful now in only one wood. A good Essex site just outside our region is Blakes Wood in the Danbury complex. From many sites in Norfolk and Suffolk, try, in the former county, the NWT reserves of Ashwellthorpe Lower Wood, Narborough Railway Line, Booton Common near Reepham, Holt Lowes and Lolly Moor or Scarning Fen near Dereham. In Suffolk there are lots of twayblade at the SWT Barton Mills Rex Graham military orchid reserve and there are plants in the marshes at Gromford, at Wortham and at the SWT reserves of Redgrave Fen, Newbourne Springs, Reydon Wood, Foxburrow Wood near Lowestoft, and in old meadows at Monewden and Metfield.

The name 'twayblade' comes from the paired 'twin' dark-green, oval, opposite leaves which are very distinctive – though occasionally it has three leaves. Its leaves have given it the alternative name of sweethearts, and people seem fond of the plant despite its unassertive green flowers, sometimes with a reddish-brown tinge.

Almost entirely restricted in this country to darkish parts of ancient or old secondary broadleaved woods on basic or neutral soils in south-east England is the violet helleborine. It was known in Norfolk up to 1910, but now avoids northern East Anglia, growing only in the southern part of West Suffolk and in north-east Essex. Oddly, it was not recorded in Suffolk until 1912, though it must have been present and is fairly easily confused with the broad-leaved helleborine, which is a little more widespread in East Anglia. The grey-green leaves of the violet helleborine are narrower and the flowers appear more white and pale than the greener-flowered forms of the broad-leaved species. One should not insist that the flowers show a violet tinge, but look instead for violet-flushed stems and leaf-bases. It occurs now in five Suffolk tetrads and can be seen in north-east Essex in Chalkney Wood and at Gestingthorpe. You can enjoy a feel of the primal East Anglian wildwood at the SWT Groton

Wood in Suffolk, where it grows beneath small-leaved lime in the oldest part of the wood. Elsewhere in Groton it is found in hazel coppice beneath oak and ash, whereas in Wolves Wood it is even more darkly covered by hornbeam coppice.

The broad-leaved helleborine is more catholic in its choice of sites. In southern England it likes beechwoods, but is found on limestone pavements in the north and west of Britain, whereas its East Anglian preferred spot is most likely to be boulder-clay ancient woodland. I almost literally stumbled on the first plant I ever saw, in deep shade in woodland at Horningtoft in Norfolk. Another Norfolk broadleaved woodland site is Honeypot Wood, though it can colonise secondary broadleaved woodland and conifer plantations. Forestry Commission plantations at Brandon and Santon Downham hold the species in quite large numbers, though more characteristically you will find only two or three plants per site, or even a plant in splendid isolation. It also occurs just across the county boundary at Santon in Norfolk and not far away at Mundford and Weeting. Nationally, this orchid of up to a metre high with a more-or-less one-sided flower-spike of anything up to a hundred flowers, is our commonest helleborine, but it is less frequent in our region and Sandford thinks it surprisingly scarce in Suffolk. The flowers tend to be pinkish in more open, drier sites but greener in dark habitats. If you are further south than Breckland, try Priestly Wood near Needham Market. In north-east Essex, it was found in Tarpey's and Heath's survey at three Sites of Special Scientific Interest and one private site, but can be seen on the EWT reserves of Little Baddow Heath and Scrubs Wood at Danbury, just outside our region.

The element of purity in the beauty of white-flowered orchid species is one attribute often denied their colourful sisters. This is particularly true of the butterfly orchids, for the coolly gracious white flowers, sometimes tinged with green, are also beautiful in their graceful long lips and spurs, their long, wavy-edged outstretched sepal-wings, their sweet fragrance and their uncluttered fewness on the stem. David Lang refers rightly to their luminous quality in dark places. As with most white-flowered species, variations in flower-structure are rare, and this constancy helps one distinguish the greater butterfly orchid from the lesser, using the flower parts, for simply relying on the former being larger than the latter is unfortunately not a reliable indicator. What one has to look at are the pollen sacs or masses, called pollinia, in the throat of the flower. In the greater butterfly, they are arranged far apart on either side of the spur in the form of an inverted V, with the tops sloping together, leaving visible the wide entrance to the spur. In the case of the lesser butterfly, the pollinia are parallel and close together, so you cannot see into the throat of the flower. These pollinia become attached to the side of the head or proboscis of visiting insects – mainly butterflies and moths – to be carried to another flower to effect fertilisation.

Though I have seen the two kinds of butterfly orchid growing together in Scotland, they have a tendency in more southern areas to prefer different habitats, thus making identification even easier. The greater butterfly is more common in East Anglia and grows very largely in calcareous woods: the Suffolk Orchid Survey turned it up in no less than 28 tetrads. Suffolk sites include Middle Wood, Ofton, Combs Wood, near Stowmarket and various other woods on the mid-Suffolk boulder clay, plus an interesting marl-pit site at Westleton. It once grew at Northfield Wood, Onehouse, though it has not been seen there recently. In north-east Essex, Tarpey's and Heath's survey revealed two sites, one with over a hundred flower spikes, and the plant can also be seen on the EWT reserve at Woodham Walter Common, Danbury. I have seen the plant recently in Norfolk at Honeypot Wood and there are other Norfolk sites including Rawhall, Horningtoft and Brooke. There are past records from Holkham, Wells, Griston, Felbrigg and Sheringham and it has also been found, a little curiously, in wet woods on acid soils south-east of King's Lynn in the 1990s. Its preference for ancient woodland sites has led to some calling it the wood butterfly orchid. It is said that it can endure deep shade and survive without flowering for two decades or more before producing further flowers when the trees are finally coppiced, though it seems to like best of all the edges of open rides.

The lesser butterfly orchid is sometimes called the field butterfly in our region. In the country as a whole, it is predominantly a plant of moorland and damp, heathy hill-pastures on acid or neutral soils, but in southern England it is also sometimes found in deep shade in beech woodland and on calcareous soils. It is much the rarer of the two butterfly orchid species in East Anglia and recent surveys failed to turn up any current sites in Suffolk and north-east Essex. Petch and Swann listed some dozen Norfolk sites in the mid-1960s, and it probably hangs on at some of them. As regards NWT reserves, I certainly saw it in the late 1980s at Roydon Common, and Upton Fen is said to be another current site.

There are other common plants of the damp, ancient, woods – the blue flowers of bugle, for instance, can be very plentiful along rides and in opened-up areas. Look especially for the fairly frequent white-flowered and rare pink-flowered forms – but let us move on to drier woods and even to unpromising coniferous plantations.

Having scent, purity and daintiness, lily-of-the-valley is a great favourite, as its presence in gardens and florists attests. Its other traditional names are also 'fancy', sometimes to the extent of seeming to include that word: liriconfancy, lily convall, Our Lady's tears, fairies' bells and ladder-to-heaven. One can see the derivation of the first two from the scientific name, *Convallaria majalis*, the May-flowering lily from (often wooded) valley-side sites that are a little drier than the valley bottoms. Even if no valley is involved, the species goes for drier woods or more gravelly soils very locally in East Anglia. Popular tradition has it that the sweet smell of the flowers drew the nightingale from the hedge to his mate in the lily-wood, but the red berries, produced only in clement years, are poisonous. In fact the entire plant is very poisonous though, medicinally, the glycosides it contains have been used to regulate heart action (like those in the foxglove), and to treat dropsy. The traditional medical applications are for apoplexy, palsy, gout, eye inflammation – and weak memory! Suffolk claims the species as the Woolpit lily.

A great rarity is the closely-related and even more diminutive May lily, which has a delicate fragrance like, but less strong than, that of the lily-of-the-valley. Each plant has, as suggested by the second element of its scientific name, *Maianthemum bifolium*, two leaves, which are heart-shaped, and a spike of very small white blossoms with conspicuous stamens, in late May and June (*Maianthemum* means 'May blossom'). The plant abounds in many north European forests, but in England it occurs only extremely locally in woods on acid soils in Durham, north-east Yorkshire, nor Lincolnshire and Norfolk. However, botanists insist that it is only 'doubtfully native' or even 'probably introduced' in East Anglia though it grows in native, mainly broadleaved woodland remote from dwellings in Swanton Great Wood. It is an erratic flowerer at its Yorkshire sites and subject to the flower heads being nibbled off by uncertainly-identified predators, but I could see no such problem at the Swanton Novers site on the visits I have been permitted to make, when the May lilies were thickly in flower. How they come to be at Swanton Novers if they are not native has long been considered a mystery, as they grow in a quite extensive patch which gives every appearance of being long established, even though a Norfolk flora of 1915 did not mention the species. However, it has been pointed out that the rhizomes are connected underground and radiate from a common origin - rather like the annular rings on a tree - which seems to be an adjacent old, large Scots pine. Possibly this was introduced from Europe, where the May lily is much more plentiful. Ian Cummings suggests a *bona-fide* researcher, permission having been granted, could calculate the age of the clone quite easily by unearthing a few radii of the shallow rhizome and counting the 'rings' (number of internodes) or ramets, and comparing the result with a calculation of the age of the pine to determine whether there is a possibility the May lilies were introduced at the same time as a seedling scots pine, or even pine seeds. There is a small Suffolk May lily colony in a mixed Victorian wood near Dunwich Common, but these are certainly introductions as other naturalised garden plants grow nearby and it has been acknowledged that they may well form part of a relic of a former semi-wild garden.

Some of the northern May lily sites are purely conifer woods, but not so in Norfolk, though there are one or two interesting flowers associated with East Anglian conifer plantations. A rare naturalised alien from central and southern Europe which, as a garden escape, has crept into coniferous and broadleaved plantations, shrubberies, waste places and even the odd churchyard is the yellow figwort. It is thinly scattered through much of Britain, but has certain East Anglian strongholds.

In Norfolk, yellow figwort is found in the north of the county around Holkham, Wells and Stiffkey and, to the south, in the Eccles and Snetterton area. In Suffolk, it has existed at Fornham St Genevieve since at least 1774, and there are clusters of sites north and east of Bury St Edmunds. The north-east Essex sites are just across the county boundary around Ardleigh, Dedham and Lawford, with a 'sprinkling' in hedges around Lawford.

The common figwort, *Scrophularia nodosa*, is, of course, much more frequent in our woods and shady places. It is the 'knotty' figwort, and the nodular rhizomes were used to treat scrofulous swellings – swellings of the neck glands – and a disease called *ficus*, which is the Latin for fig; hence 'figwort'. Another interesting figwort which sometimes grows in damp woodland as well as in shaded spots on stream- and river-banks, and in marshes and fens, is the green figwort, which was first recorded as a rarity in Norfolk in 1904, but has now increased greatly in various parts of the country and is locally frequent in parts of our region. It is like common figwort, but the stem is broadly winged and the sharply-toothed leaves are narrowed at the base, and it differs from water figwort in that the leaves of the latter are blunt-toothed.

You would not expect an orchid at home in the remnants of the ancient Caledonian pine forests on Speyside to figure in an account of East Anglian flowers at all, yet the creeping lady's-tresses flowers in July and August in at least two north Norfolk conifer plantations. It occurs at Holkham under the Corsican pines planted in the 19th century to stabilise the dunes, and I have seen it in conifers at Holt Country Park, formerly the Old Racecourse. It appeared at various other locations between 1885 and the 1960s, including other sites in the Holt area, Westwick, Bodham, Cawston and Cranwich. A colony certainly still thrives in the Norfolk Breck in the Emily's Wood area. This cluster of Norfolk sites for an orchid that has otherwise penetrated no further south than Durham and Cumbria is intriguing, and botanists are almost convinced that it is an established or naturalised alien, probably introduced in soil clinging to pine seedlings brought from Scotland. There are two 1930s Suffolk records for the SWT Stuston Common, which is puzzling as there are no conifer plantations there. Creeping lady's-tresses likes ground cover of moist, rotting pine needles through which it can develop roots, leaves and, after turning upwards, flowering stems. The leaves are conspicuously net-veined. The thin, hairy stem produces what is really a spiral of flowers, though all the rather sickly-fragrant, creamy-white flowers turn to face the same way.

East Anglia, with so much land long-devoted or recently turned-over to arable farming, has hardly been an exception to the national trend of the substantial grubbing-out of hedgerows since World War II. Much of the region comprises what Oliver Rackham calls the 'Ancient Countryside' of lowland England with, among other rural features, a tendency to mixed, sinuous, centuries-old hedgerows, though north and west Norfolk and the Breck are largely part of Rackham's 'Planned Countryside', where hedges are more modern, straight and species-poor, usually not dating back further than the 'Parliamentary' enclosures of the 18th and 19th centuries.

The subject of the origin and history of our ancient hedgerows is as complex as that of our old woods, and Oliver Rackham has dealt with it fascinatingly: suffice it to say here that however rich and historic they are, there are now many fewer of them. This was well illustrated in Norfolk's case as long ago as 1970 when aerial photographs were taken of the same 16% of the land surface of the county that had also been photographed by the RAF in 1946. Varied countryside and soils were involved and the rate of disappearance of hedges in the intervening quarter-century was uneven, but overall some 45% or 8,000 miles of hedges had been destroyed. Although the Ministry of Agriculture stopped subsidising hedge removal in 1972, figures released in 1994 suggested no slackening of the national hedge removal rate in the decade to 1993 and we have certainly lost half our hedgerows in these parts of Norfolk. The situation is not really reassuringly better further south in the region: about a third of the hedges have been removed from a substantial area of north Essex since World War II in the move to larger wheat and rape fields.

Hedges, of course, take time and money to trim and maintain, and the bigger and thicker and richer they are, the more of the farmer's land they take up and shade out. They have often lost their function of penning in beasts and remain only as boundary markers or for landscape amenity purposes. But it costs money to grub them up too, and, as they provide cover, sporting rights are also worth something on many a farm. Of the hedgerows that survive, a growing number are totally neglected and many others either degraded and gappy through merciless flailing or kept perpetually so trimmed and thinned as to be hardly there at all. This last must be distinguished from an older practice here and there of treating a hedge as a strip of coppiced woodland by cutting it to ground level every 10 years whilst leaving some trees untouched to grow on as standards (or re-lopping old pollards). Saplings in such a regime can be tagged with plastic markers to prevent their being flailed. There has been much criticism recently of the tendency to 'tidy' hedgerows constantly during slack times of the agricultural year so potential standard trees never grow on from the existing hedge species. This tidying urge can be resisted and money saved in the process, but a more discriminating, sympathetic maintenance of our remaining hedgerows and the consequent nurturing of associated plants and other wildlife seems to appeal still only to a minority of farmers and landowners.

As well as a host of common wayside flowers, there are a few unusual plants to be found in East Anglian hedgerows. Some interesting grassland species that happen also to grow on roadside verges have been referred to in the first chapter so attention here can be focused on one or two rarities more closely associated with the shrubs and trees themselves. One such is the scarce crested cow-wheat, an annual of the lousewort tribe, with handsome yellow and purple flowers and prominently serrated or toothed leafy bracts, justifying the 'crested' epithet. One thinks of it as a native of old, often oak woodland clearings, rides and borders, and of scrub on the chalky boulder clay, but it cropped up as a roadside-verge species in a Norfolk survey of the 1970s, and a number of its remaining East Anglian sites are on hedgebanks and verges that once bordered woodland. In Norfolk, it seems to have crossed the road from its long-established site at the edge of Rawhall Wood, and now hangs on by the skin of its teeth on the opposite verge. The best site I have seen in Suffolk is again at the foot of a hedge and along a quite wide grassy verge at the Suffolk Wildlife Trust roadside verge reserve at Hargrave, and it occurs on another SWT roadside verge reserve at Great Whelnetham. The species is described by the botanists as decreasing throughout its range, which is very much East Anglia and immediately adjacent counties to the west, though it was once more widespread. It is extinct at many former Suffolk sites, though it was still present in six parishes in the early 1980s, and *Scarce Plants* records it in some two dozen tetrads since 1970 in West Suffolk and part of north Essex outside our region. There was one north-east Essex record in 1724, but it has not been found in the area since. It has been recorded in only one Norfolk tetrad since 1970, though it formerly grew elsewhere in central north Norfolk in two hectads. I seem fated, despite local guidance, not to see it at any of its old wood-border sites to the west such as Castor Hanglands near Peterborough, and I have also been unlucky with some of its alleged Cambridgeshire haunts, such as Hayley Wood, west of Cambridge.

Even the so-called common cow-wheat is now an uncommon plant in our region. It grows plentifully beneath the pines of many ancient Scottish woods and on the open heath, but in East Anglia it is found in woodland clearings, thickets and woody lanes on the clay. Rarest of all, though, is the vivid magenta-and-gold field cow-wheat, *Melampyrum arvense,* which once grew in Norfolk cornfields and is still found in Essex on one cornfield edge only, but outside the north-east of the county, though it was recorded long ago at Wickham Bishops and Witham. What a pity it is so rare in England: I have seen it in profusion at the foot of the wire mesh boundary fence of a new French motorway picnic area, as if keen to break in and repossess the appropriated land.

The *melas* of *Melampyrum* means black, *pyros* is wheat, and the two together refer to the seed which is about the size of a wheat grain, and the fact it turns flour black when ground and mixed in with it. Cows are said to be appropriately fond of cow-wheat and Linnaeus assures us it produces the yellowest butter.

There is some uncertainty whether the stinking hellebore is an East Anglian native, though current botanical opinion pronounces it 'probably native' in some other parts of the country, and considers it most likely to have been introduced in our region. It is familiar enough, however, to have acquired the local name setterwort in Suffolk, where it grows on chalk or chalky boulder clay in hedges and thickets, and sometimes simply setter in Norfolk. Handsome plants can be seen in flower as early as February on the roadside bank below the church at Flixton in Suffolk, though it also grows more plentifully in appropriate olfactory association with abundant stinking iris just across the Waveney on the wooded slopes of the Bath Hills at Ditchingham. The plant is popular in gardens, but, curiously, it seems that the purplish-maroon edges to the lime-green sepals nearly always desert it when it is cultivated. The stems, which persist from one spring to the next, stink pretty dreadfully when crushed. The green hellebore, known as bear's foot, is probably a rare naturalised alien and grows in woods and copses on loamy or chalky soils. Apparently, cattle were once blessed with hellebores, ritually dug up. The stinking and green hellebores were once used as a violent remedy against worms in children, but, as the plants are 'drastically, dangerously and poisonously cathartic', the treatment sometimes killed the patient!

Let us finish with a plant we associate with Christmas and the end of the year. I cannot claim it as a 'flower' in the everyday sense, nor is it really a hedgerow plant, for it grows on trees, wild and domestic, in a variety of situations. You have, of course, guessed it to be the mystic mistletoe, which actually flowers inconspicuously in February to April, but berries from November through December. It is native in East Anglia, living semi-parasitically on various species of tree: hawthorn, apple, balsam poplar, lime, ash, maple, elm, oak, plum, whitethorn, hazel, willow and medlar have all been recorded as hosts. There is a recent report of its growing on a cotoneaster in a Gloucestershire garden and an old Irish occurrence on a willow-stump gatepost, so possibly the BSBI Mistletoe Survey, underway as I write, will turn up some new and curious East Anglian hosts. Oddly, mistletoe has very few English local names, but amongst them are masslin in Suffolk and mislin-bush more generally in East Anglia. It is now rare to infrequent in much of the region, particularly Norfolk, though Simpson considered it frequent but less common than of old in Suffolk. It is more a shrub of the west of the country, being common on the English/Welsh borders and in Worcestershire apple orchards.

The mistle-thrush gets his name from feeding on the berries, but the world 'mistletoe' itself comes from the Old English *misteltan*, the meaning of which remains a mystery, very appropriate to a plant of strange powers and significances since druidical times: there was much ritual and mumbo-jumbo surrounding the ceremonial gathering of it into white cloths with golden knives, preferably from oak trees, which are rare hosts. Its evergreen nature perhaps makes it an unsurprising midwinter associate with holly and ivy, but it was also included in the traditional garland of Jack-in-the-green, the ritual figure symbolising the return of summer. We all appreciate the licence-to-kiss that it grants (it is traditionally an aphrodisiac and helps women conceive), but it exudes a wider benevolence when hung above the threshold, symbolising hospitality and peace and protecting against storms and all evil. It should be preserved through the year as a potent witch-repellent at Hallowe'en and protector of babes from fairies who would substitute a changeling. It will magically open a lock and divine hidden treasure. There is lots more. The North American Indians were less fey about it and made mistletoe tea to treat measles, toothache and dog bites. It has been used in proprietary medicines for hypertension, and as a tonic.

ABOVE: False oxlip. BELOW: Lesser celandine.

LEFT: Wood spurge. RIGHT: Wood anemone.

ABOVE: Moschatel. LEFT: Wood sorrel. RIGHT: Ramsons.

LEFT: Bugle. RIGHT: Water avens. BELOW: Herb paris.

ABOVE: Crested cow-wheat. BELOW: Sweet woodruff.

LEFT: Yellow figwort by a church wall. RIGHT: Violet helleborine.

ABOVE: Stinking hellebore. BELOW: Mistletoe on New Year's Day.

February snowdrops and a band of winter aconites, Aldborough, Norfolk.

LEFT: Columbine. RIGHT: Marsh pea.

Wetland Wildflowers

> What would the world be, once bereft
> Of wet and of wildness? Let them be left,
> O let them be left, wildness and wet;
> Long live the weeds and the wilderness yet.
>
> Gerard Manley Hopkins

East Anglia, one of the driest English regions as regards annual rainfall, figures as a decidedly watery place in the nation's imagination. This paradox arises of course from the popular identification of the Broads with the area as a whole, and perhaps from hazy memories of school lessons on crown jewels lost in the Wash and the difficulties posed by the Fens to access from the west, midlands and north in the days of Hereward the Wake. But it is true that our largely low-lying counties of slow and once freely-overbrimming rivers still possess a wide range of wetland plant habitats, though their numbers have reduced alarmingly. Our liquid assets are not limited to the streams and rivers with their aquatic and marginal vegetation: there are also the Broadland fens and far-reaching grazing marshes and drainage dykes; the valley bogs, wet heaths and fens of the higher reaches of the river systems, and such wet meadows as survive; the brackish Suffolk lagoons and mysterious Breckland meres outside Broadland; and, on the western edge of our region, a slice of that remarkable part of the Fens known as the Ouse Washes.

So widespread are East Anglian wet places that the commoner wetland plants have in the past competed with wayside flowers for public recognition and affection. Their distinguishing characteristics, together with their virtues and efficacies, dangers and menaces, are woven into the history of our life and customs. A short plant list makes the point: lady's-smock, meadowsweet, May blobs, loosestrife, ragged Robin and brandy-bottle.

Lady's-smock, so-called from the fancied resemblance of the lilac or whitish flowers to such garments hanging out to dry, and traditionally associated with wanton young women, has dozens of local names throughout Britain, including cuckoo-flower in Norfolk and Suffolk, as it blooms on the return of that bird in the springtime. Shakespeare, drawing on Gerard's *Herbal* of 1597 in *Love's Labour's Lost*, describes the colour as 'all silver white' as the plants 'paint the meadows with delight'. Cuckoo-flowers are also milkmaids in Suffolk and Essex and, less attractively folksy, pigs' eyes in the latter county. Curiously, they were known as headaches in Cambridgeshire, which is another name for the common poppy in other counties. Two local names for lady's-smock bound to cause confusion had they not more or less died out are paigle in Suffolk, normally applied to the cowslip, and water lily in Norfolk, normally applied to water lilies! The peppery young leaves of lady's-smock are cress-like and cress-tasting, but apparently the flowers should not be gathered for the vase from its wet woodland and grazed or mown wet-meadow sites, as it is a plant of the fairies, unlucky in the house.

The ragged Robin, sometimes called ragged Jack in Essex, with its seemingly tattered, red-pink flowers, has similar avian associations: the specific elements of its scientific name, *Lychnis floc-cuculi*, mean 'flower of the cuckoo'. Swallowtail butterflies in Broadland are certainly attracted to it.

The intense perfume of meadowsweet is the very fragrance of wetland high summers and its creamy, frothy flowers can be added to a number of drinks to impart a sweet, pleasant flavour. Meadowsweet tea, made from the flowers, is supposed to be good for influenza and feverish conditions, and for rheumatism and dropsy. The plant was cut for hay to give the cattle a treat in less pitilessly-efficient agricultural times and can be smoked like tobacco. Its common name goes back to Saxon days when it was the mede-or or medo-wyrt (the mead- or honey-herb), used to give mead – and later claret and port – an aromatic bouquet, and its elm-like leaves explain the second element of its scientific name, *Filipendula ulmaria*. Sweet is as sweet does, so it is surprising to find countervailing darker attributes: some traditions claim meadowsweet can cause fits, or associate it with death, asserting the power of its scent to induce a sleep so deep you may never awaken. And there is a puzzling contradiction between the fact the Elizabethans strewed their floors with meadowsweet and its reputation as yet another plant threatening ill-luck if brought into the house.

May blobs (or Mary's buds) are of course marsh marigolds or kingcups, still quite widely found in marshes and wet woods, and beside ditches, streams, rivers and ponds. Like lady's-smock, the marsh marigold has a host of English local names. As for its scientific binominal, *Caltha Palustris* derives in part from *kalathos*, a goblet, which is appropriate to its generously cupped flowers, usually of a bright, solid shade of yellow – though they are occasionally lemon coloured. The kingcup has been used for curing rashes and the petals yield a yellow dye.

Loosestrife, it was said, quietens savage beasts, especially agitated horses and oxen. Our river and stream-sides are blessed with both the purple kind, *Lythrum salicaria* (*Lythrum* is from the Greek word for blood), which repels flies and gnats in the home, and the unrelated bright yellow loosestrife, which is rendered even more attractive when blue damsel-flies hover over its flowers. The gypsies used an infusion of yellow loosestrife leaves to cure diarrhoea. Spikes of purple loosestrife have been called soldiers in Norfolk and some have thought that Shakespeare's reference to 'Long Purples' in *Hamlet* indicates purple loosestrife (or even the lords-and-ladies or cuckoo-pint), though almost certainly he meant the early-purple orchid.

Other yellow flowers we see commonly in East Anglian wet places are that handsome iris, the yellow flag, sometimes called fligger in our region, and the yellow water-lily. The rhizomes of the yellow iris yield a black dye and ink and the roasted seeds are alleged to make a coffee-like hot beverage. But this rhizome is poisonous and some folk traditions assert that gnawing the plant will make you stammer! Children make toy sailing boats from the leaves. The yellow water-lily bears 'brandy-bottle' fruiting capsules later in the season, but establishes its bibbing associations earlier by producing flowers giving a faint whiff of alcoholic drink. Unlike the white water-lily, the yellow species can anchor itself unshiftably in the moving water of rivers, though powerboat propellers pose a stiffer challenge. The yellow water-lily can endure fairly muddy conditions, but it does not rival its white-flowered sister in tolerating to a degree enriched and polluted still water. The dried rootstock of the white water lily has seen medicinal use as a heart tonic.

In surveying East Anglian wetlands and their flowers, it is usual to start with Broadland and I shall make no perverse divergence from tradition here. The broads, those reed- or carr-fringed lakes of east Norfolk and a limited area of north-east Suffolk, are flooded medieval peat-diggings on an impressive scale. Some are linked directly to the main rivers of the area, others are isolated from them. The waters that feed into the system are influenced by underlying chalk or the chalky boulder clay, so the freshwater broads and Broadland rivers tend to be naturally basic with a pH usually above eight. The Thurne broads are slightly brackish. The broads are shallow (Cockshoot was down to less than six inches in places before much mud was pumped out in 1982) and more than two-thirds of the original area of water has filled itself in through the centuries, though there remain some 125 miles of navigable waters and broads. Leaving aside human intervention for a moment, the broads are, of course, subject to the natural process of succession. Typically, open water is encroached upon by the fringing reedswamp, which in turn creates conditions for colonisation by sedges and swamp carr of alder and sallow. Eventually, mixed carr or wet woodland of oak, ash and birch may follow.

The ecological crisis of the Broads that is still so sadly current has stolen up on us through this century. Before then, the broads were famous for their clear waters and low-growing carpets of water weeds. But an increasing input of phosphates from sewage effluent, combined with nitrates from farmland fertilisers introduced by 'run off' into the rivers, has produced enriched waters that stimulate an initial luxuriant growth of water weeds and increased fish populations, followed by microscopic algae proliferating in their millions. It is thought that nitrate levels in East Anglia this century have been the highest in the country.

By the 1950s, the waters were going cloudy and turbid with a 'soup' of algae which formed an oozy mud on the bottom as they died, increasing the sedimentation rate. By the 1970s, the Broads were suffering ecological and environmental degradation as bad as anywhere, with the aquatic vegetation in most broads and the middle and lower reaches of the rivers in terminal decline or – mostly – gone altogether. Barton Broad's flowering aquatic plants diminished from 11 to none between 1911 and 1972 and by the early 1970s 11 of 28 broads surveyed similarly lacked flowering aquatics – and most of the remainder had only the tenacious yellow water-lily. The Thurne Broads were still relatively well flowered, but decreasing diversity soon became the rule here also. Only Calthorpe, Martham South and Upton Broads – all with limited or no inflow from agricultural land – retained any of the magic of the old broads.

The intensity of recreational use of the Broads by motor cruisers did not help the situation. Uncushioned now by stable mats of water plants at the edge of broads and unprotected by a flourishing range of plants rooted in them, banks were eroded by up to three metres a year in some particularly vulnerable places.

In 1978, the Countryside Commission prompted local councils to form the Broads Authority and a programme of research and restoration got under way. In March 1988, the Broads Bill received its royal assent and the Broads Authority now at last had statutory powers – including, crucially, control over navigation – to attempt the ecological resuscitation of Broadland. The area is now a national park in all but name. The varied projects to date, before and after the Broads Act, have included the mud-pumping of some broads, the installing of phosphorus-extraction plant in sewage works, experimentation with different methods of protecting banks and restoring marginal and bank vegetation, the clearing of dykes and scrub, the imposition of speed limits on boats and some movement towards hull designs causing less turbulence, and even research into algae-consuming waterfleas and other biomanipulative techniques. Reviving the whole system, however, even over a long period, remains a daunting challenge which we cannot be certain is realisable despite some heartening successes and increasingly ambitious projects.

In the case of Broadland fens (essentially reeds and sedges on spongy, peaty soil flushed with base-rich water), the problem was that regular cutting for thatching or hay had largely ceased, the process of succession had turned many formerly open fens to wet woodland, and wooded river valleys had developed over a wide area, in particular along the Bure. Fen plants were shaded out and dykes became overgrown and defunct. Many fens had also been drained and lost to farming. The Broads Authority responded by offering advice, grant aid and even a labour supply to help restore private fens. Some areas of Broadland are also national, county wildlife trust, or local reserves managed in traditional ways by the bodies responsible, and the fens here are safer, though farming practices and water extraction on surrounding land can and sometimes do still threaten such reserves.

Of the extensive Broadland grazing marshes, it has been estimated that some 25% have been deep-drained and ploughed since 1970 and kept in arable by means of ultra-efficient electric pumps. A policy of subsidising farmers in designated 'Environmentally Sensitive Areas' to manage marshes in traditional ways was eventually implemented. The preservation of grazing marsh systems was vitally important for wetland plants, for the grids of drainage dykes had become refuges for many species rare in the broads and rivers or banished from them. Drainage dykes silt up rapidly and dredging them in rotation every five or 10 years so that organic mud is removed is a farming practice that actually maintains the diversity of species.

The loss-rate of grazing marshes and other wetland habitats in the rest of the region has been no lower. In Suffolk, for instance, it is said that over 60% of grazing marshes have been lost or damaged since the 1940s, largely by drainage, 'improvement' and a switch to cereal growing from dairy and beef cattle farming. Half of all the plant species lost in Suffolk have been aquatics, marginals or wetlanders.

In Barnby Broad, Fritton Lake and Flixton Decoy, Suffolk has three Norfolk-type broads. The county also possesses its own kind of natural brackish broad in the shape of Oulton, Easton, Covehithe and Benacre Broads, which are the estuaries of small rivers dammed up by sand and shingle bars: sea-shells have been brought up in dyke-dredgings at Oulton and the encroaching sea, a threat all along the coast between Lowestoft and Southwold, has killed trees at Benacre and sometimes breaks into these former estuaries. Other coastal lagoons take the form of pools in the shingle, as at Shingle Street, or clay-bottomed shallow pools on old marshland cut off behind the shingle, as at Dunwich.

There are relics of formerly-large inland meres in the shape of the SWT Framlingham Mere, and Cornard Mere near Sudbury; in the Decoy Ponds near Bixley Heath; and in Rushmere near Ipswich. North-east Essex has no natural lakes, though it does possess reservoirs which are increasingly important for wildlife. Even many Essex ponds have suffered a lamentable decline into willow-filled hollows, or have been filled with rubbish and surfaced with top soil. Suffolk, despite also losing many of its ponds, is said to have more still than any other English county: certainly, north and central Suffolk, with south and mid Norfolk, were estimated to have ponds thicker on the ground than anywhere else in lowland England in the 1920s. The trouble is that ponds require attention to retain varied plant communities, but many have been neglected since farms started to use piped water, so that they became choked with organic matter and silt, and sometimes shaded by surrounding trees and scrub.

Plant recording for the recent North-east Essex Flora Project confirmed that the canalisation of rivers, the piping of streams and creation of culverts, and the undue deepening and re-cutting of ditches to give steeper sides, had proceeded apace. Also, arable farming now tends to be carried out right to the brink of north-east Essex rivers, leaving few marshy margins for wetland plants. None of Suffolk's rivers remain in their natural state: all, to a greater or lesser degree, have been canalised, dammed, diverted, dredged, or cut by weirs and locks so that features necessary if a variety of plants are to thrive – low cliffs, bays, meanders, shoals, riffles and wet shelves at the margins – have often been damaged or destroyed. To compound the problems, river flows have been reduced by water abstraction and, of course, water quality has been affected by sewage and industrial effluent discharges and by agricultural practices. The result is impoverishment across the range of river and river-bank habitats: fewer sheets of water crowfoot in mid-stream; fewer plants of arrowhead and flowering rush in the shallow water at the edge; fewer gently-shelving, cattle-trodden banks to support brooklime, celery-leaved buttercup and the water forget-me-not. However, the National Rivers Authority has in recent years embraced its conservation role by working towards recreating, where it considers it possible, good riverside conditions for wildlife.

The Broadland carrs, subject to flooding, are poor in flowering plant species, though they do sometimes contain climbers and scramblers such as hop, black bindweed, honeysuckle and woody nightshade, or bittersweet. So let us move straight to consider some of the more interesting flowering plants characteristic of fens, marshes and other wetland habitats. Fens boast a greater number of species than probably any other habitat, and the composition of the flora varies somewhat from fen to fen, in part dependent on the degree and kind of management that is in place. Broadland fens may be of the flood-plain type fed principally by river water, but Norfolk and Suffolk also have valley fens which are fed in the main by springs and seepage from the valley sides, and here too the communities of flowering plants may vary subtly in composition and disposition.

Orchids have a good claim to be the particular glory of fens, and of wetlands more generally. The marsh orchids of the genus *Dactylorhiza* are possibly our showiest species after the military orchid. The name comes from two Greek words, *dactylos*, a finger, and *rhiza*, a root, and the orchids have pale, lobed tubers like hands and fingers (common spotted orchids are dead man's fingers in Somerset), though it must be admitted they are rather flat, squashed fingers in some species.

The early marsh-orchid, sometimes called the meadow orchid, is my favourite of the genus; partly because the first flower spikes grace our wetland sites a couple of weeks before the commoner southern marsh orchid, but also because it comes in a range of shades – colours indeed – which outshine the dowdier hues of the lilac-mauve forms of the southern or common marsh-orchid, though the latter can be purple or dark magenta. The early marsh is particularly attractive when, true to the specific element of its scientific name, *Dactylorhiza incarnata*, its flowers are a pale, fairly pure flesh-pink, with red to dark-purple loops, lines and dots. There are darker and also creamy-white forms. It prefers alkaline-to-neutral fens, marshes, bogs, wet meadows and pastures, and even damp dune slacks, but is scarcer than this list of habitats suggests and rarely appears in large numbers, though I did recently see what could be termed without undue exaggeration a 'small fieldful' in an unimproved, rushy meadow in Norfolk's Upper Tas Valley. Other Norfolk sites include the NWT Thompson Common, Upton Fen and Holme Dunes reserves, and the Suffolk Orchid Survey recorded the species in some 26 tetrads since 1980, with its strongholds identified as fens in the Waveney/Little Ouse Valley and Lothingland, as coastal marshes around Sizewell, and as Breckland fens near Lakenheath and Mildenhall. There are some SWT reserves on which it may be seen: a now-thriving colony in the Norah Hanbury-Kelk Memorial Meadows near Mildenhall; a few plants at North Cove near Barnby; colonies in Butcher's Marsh and Camps Heath Marshes near Oulton Broad. There are no recent records of the early marsh orchid in north-east Essex. Those who become orchidophiles will also wish to see the more interesting subspecies of *Dactylorhiza incarnata*. Subspecies *coccinea* for instance – a vividly vermilion or crimson form like a dumpy hyacinth – grows only in Ireland, Scotland, Wales and the Isle of Man – and Norfolk! It may be sought along the spring-line in the Sidestrand/Overstrand district. Subspecies *ochroleuca*, with its pale straw-yellow flowers featuring large, unmarked, three-lobed lips, is the real East Anglian dactylorchid speciality, but is now rare in Norfolk and Suffolk to what seems the point of disappearance. It was still at the SWT Redgrave Fen in 1987 and the *Orchids of Suffolk* avers that any plants remaining there are probably the last in the county.

   The southern marsh is the most widespread and abundant marsh orchid in East Anglia, so much so that there are really too many sites to list. Martin Sanford's book provides a good Suffolk selection, to which one might add the SWT reserves of Market Weston Fen, Darsham Marshes and Lakenheath Poors Fen. In Norfolk, try the NWT reserves of Holme Dunes, Holt Lowes, Lolly Moor and the old borrow-pits next to the Narborough Railway Embankment, though there are lots more. There are at least three north-east Essex sites – at Belchamp Water and the EWT reserves of Chigborough Lakes and Loshes Meadows. There is some overlap of flowering-season with the early marsh orchid and some colour forms of each species are not dissimilar, but the early marsh has a narrow, reflexed flower lip, whereas the southern marsh's entire or shallowly three-loped lip is broader, with a paler area at its centre marked with tiny dots but never a double loop. There are varieties or subspecies of the southern marsh, including the so-called leopard marsh orchid with heavily ring-spotted leaves (variety or subspecies *junialis*, or sometimes *pardalina*!) which is the dominant form in some Suffolk meadows at Brightwell. And there is another dactylorchid species with only seven-to-twelve flowers per spike, sometimes called the Irish marsh orchid (which slights the other parts of the British Isles in which it is found) and sometimes Pugsley's or Traunsteiner's orchid (both of which are ugly); so I think we may fix upon its other, usually accurate if uninspired name of narrow-leaved marsh orchid. It likes saturated conditions in calcareous fens and has died out at many East Anglian sites, despite the region being one of its strongholds. Perhaps the drying-out fens so common today are the explanation, and there have also been suggestions that the species hybridizes easily with the southern marsh orchid. I have found Norfolk narrow-leaved marsh orchids without too much searching and uncertainty at Beeston Bog near Sheringham, and it can be seen in Suffolk at Coney Weston Fen and at Eastbridge, near Minsmere. But at some sites, such as Market Weston Fen in Suffolk and Foulden Common in Norfolk, one finds a continuum of orchids from southern marsh to narrow-leaved marsh.

   Amateur botanists turning to orchids should be forewarned: those of the genus *Dactylorhiza* have, presumably, become differentiated as species only relatively recently in evolutionary terms, and it is thus difficult to define the closely-related and often variable species and subspecies, even when they do not interbreed. A whole spectrum of intermediate forms can be found. Almost any hybrid between any two marsh-orchid species, or between any marsh-orchid and a spotted orchid may from time to time occur, not to mention dactylorchid crosses with fragrant orchids. It may further perplex new orchid fans intent on losing themselves in the agonies and the ecstacies of dactylorchid differentiation to known that recent work by some plant geneticists on southern marsh orchids suggests to them that a clutch of British and European marsh dactylorchid species should perhaps be regarded all as subspecies of a single variable species, *Dactylorhiza majalis*. This has been hitherto the scientific name for the western marsh orchid, unknown in East Anglia!

To see – and sniff – the fragrant or scented orchid itself, East Anglians need to travel to the western reaches of our region to find it in its dry chalk grassland habitat along the Devil's Dyke which runs across the racecourses of Newmarket Heath. But the marsh fragrant orchid – that is, the subspecies *densiflora* of the fragrant orchid – is much more accessible, growing in Norfolk calcareous fens and marshes such as Buxton Heath and the NWT reserves of Booton Common and Lolly Moor. It can also be found in four or five Suffolk Waveney fens, including Redgrave, Thelnetham, Hopton and Market Weston. It has a densely-packed, 30-60cm-high spike of flowers, which have a slight lilac tinge not characteristic of that other unmarked pink orchid, the pyramidal. Fragrant orchids live up to their name magnificently, with a powerful vanilla scent which may, when they grow in such numbers that you can surround yourself with them, overpower locally the fenny smell of their habitat and fill the air voluptuously on warm, still days in July or early August. Some compare the scent to that of carnations, but possibly it loses some of its sweetness within a few days of the flowers having opened. The flowers, and their long, curving spurs filled with nectar, attract moths, butterflies and bees.

My own favourite orchid of calcareous fens is the marsh helleborine, which is not unlike a miniature version of the exotic orchids, particularly the *Cymbidiums*, that garden centres sell to customers to grow in their conservatories. But the marsh helleborine grows bravely in the East Anglian open air, and Norfolk is arguably its national heartland. The fairly lax, one-sided flower spikes usually carry up to 20 flowers, decreasing in size up the stem, between July and early September, and the creeping, rhizomatous root system can give rise to a number of stems. The flowers have white, pink, yellow, brownish and red-purple elements in their colouring and their beauty repays close examination, especially the frilly, whitish lip with a central yellow blotch. Nationally, they are probably most often found in dune slacks. In Norfolk, they grow, among other places, at Upton Fen, Booton Common, Buxton Heath, Lolly Moor, Scarning Fen and Smallburgh Fen. Suffolk sites are few – three or four in the Waveney Valley – try Market Weston Fen. There is a variety, usually called var. *ochroleuca*, which lacks the red-brown pigments and is unknown in Suffolk, but has in its time been recorded in Norfolk at Beeston Bog and Burnham Overy Staithe.

Much less spectacular, but perhaps more notable because it is a national rarity, is the fen orchid itself, which has been recorded in calcareous or neutral fens in Norfolk, Suffolk and Cambridgeshire, and in dune slacks in Devon, Carmarthenshire and Glamorgan. The East Anglian plants differ in having longer leaves in relation to their breadth than the more oval-shaped leaves of the western race. The few green flowers on a lax spike appear in June and July and the small yellow-green plant is difficult to discern despite being slightly brighter than the surrounding reeds and the moss carpet in which it usually grows. Reed-cutting and wetter seasons seem to induce better flowerings. Sometimes, fen orchids grow on tussocks of fibrous tussock sedge as epiphytes (that is, they derive no nutrients from the host plant). Though seed is produced, the fen orchid can reproduce by vegetative multiplication by means of the two hard pseudobulbs that develop from the base of the stem which may separate and grow on into new plants.

The fen orchid has prospered in its western sites, but declined disastrously in East Anglia because of the draining and cultivation of fens and from lack of management leading to some sites becoming overgrown with scrub. Once there were 16 sites, but the species has been lost from Suffolk and Cambridgeshire and hangs on precariously in East Norfolk, where two principal sites remain in the Ant Valley, with one or two lesser Broadland stations. Current locations are, wisely, not revealed to general enquirers by English Nature, and photographers have been asked to restrict their attentions to plants in the west of the country for the moment. Even so, the orchid's survival must be in doubt, though English Nature recently awarded the Norfolk Wildlife Trust a contract under its Species Recovery Programme to manage more effectively areas of suitable habitat and to increase them, and to re-establish the fen orchid on some sites from which it has been lost. Plants grown from seed in Kew greenhouses by scientists of the Sainsbury Orchid Project are being used: the first Norfolk plantings were made in 1995. We must keep our fingers crossed.

In passing, an orchid even rarer in our region, though not desperately scarce in its strongholds in Scotland and the New Forest, should be mentioned. If the fen orchid is difficult to discern, seeking out the bog orchid makes searching for needles in haystacks a brief warm-up exercise. It is not just that its flowers are similarly yellow-green and inconspicuous, as is the plant as a whole, but this is also the smallest British orchid species, growing often no more than 5cm high. It prefers saturated, acid conditions in cushions of sphagnum moss, which again makes it difficult to spot, and it is an erratic flowerer. One is likely – or rather, unlikely – to find it now in very small numbers only in a single valley mire in north-west Norfolk, where I have seen only one plant. Before 1970, it had been present at one time or another in some eight 10-kilometre squares in East Anglia. At Bryants Heath near Felmingham in Norfolk, it was last seen as long ago as 1945 (Felthorpe was another former site), and it has not been seen in Suffolk for over a hundred years. If you know the remaining Norfolk site, please refrain from exploring the fragile habitat: the warden has been exasperated in recent years by the trampling of such plants as there are by people unsuccessfully searching for them! The bog orchid is unusual in that it is more common in Britain than across its continental European range, where it is considered a threatened species.

The flowers of the bog orchid, which appear in July and through August into September, are tiny and 'upside down', with the lip at the top. They are said to be pollinated by small flies, which must indeed be minute, and the seeds float on the water for dispersal. But the bog orchid also propagates itseld by producing bulbils on the margin and apex of its two-to-five leaves, which, though small, are not difficult to discern. The bulbils in time become detached and new plants may develop from them.

Even if the orchids were to be subtracted from the flora of fens, much splendour and variety would remain. Some order has been imposed on the rampant plenitude of fen species by grouping a number as 'tall-herb communities', including such flowering plants as valerian, angelica, meadowsweet, hemp agrimony, yellow and purple loosestrife and marsh thistle; and others, as 'low-herb communities', which include fen bedstraw, marsh valerian, meadow thistle, marsh lousewort (or red-rattle), grass of Parnassus and Devilsbit scabious, as well as the wetland orchid species.

My own favourite in these lists is the grass of Parnassus, though one has to wait until after midsummer for the stunning beauty of its delicately-veined, ivory-white flowers, its heart-shaped leaves and its restrained honey-sweet scent. Ted Ellis referred to the glistening perfection and waxen fragility of the blooms and exaggerated not a whit. Inspiring it may be, but this species is a nothern temperate zone plant which does not in fact grace Mount

Marsh marigold by a drainage dyke, Eaton Marshes, Norwich.

Parnassus and its Muses. It is always a local plant in Britain and is very rare or absent altogether in the south of England. I have seen it growing in dune slacks in north-west England, but the short stems in the exposed position there gave the plants a stubbiness which made them less attractive than the taller forms more characteristic of inland East Anglia. In our region, it is a plant mainly of alkaline fens, marshes and even old wet pastures, though it seems to like particularly areas where fen begins to give way to bog. It is more common in Norfolk than elsewhere in the region, being rare and decreasing in Suffolk and absent from north-east Essex.

Apparently, an infusion of the leaves of grass of Parnassus is good for digestive problems and liver complaints, but please stick to the liver salts and do not pick this delightful rarity. You can see it at Holt Lowes, Scarning and Smallburgh Fens, and Roydon Comon in Norfolk (all NWT), at Market Weston and Thelnetham Fens in Suffolk (SWT), and at Redgrave and Lopham Fen (also SWT), which straddles the boundary between the two counties.

Grass of Parnassus grows at Buxton Heath north of Norwich in close proximity to a more common plant, *Succisia pratensis*, the Devilsbit scabious or, in our region, bundweed, which some say prefers acid grassland and heath, but which is in fact remarkable for its catholic taste in habitats; nationally, you can find it in grassy places which may be acidic, wet, shady, chalky, dry, or open, in any possible combination. Its bluish-violet (occasionally pinkish-lilac) pincushion flowers are quite attractive, but it is the plant's name that claims attention as much as anything. The scientific generic name provides the first clue: *Succisia* is from the Latin and means 'broken off' or 'cut off below' – a reference to the abruptly-shortened root. There are at least two explanations of why the Devil took a bite from it: first, he was angry that the long root could cure almost anything; second, it was a case of the displacement of his anger from its true target, the Virgin Mary, who had nullified the power derived from this potent root that he was exercising.

A speciality of Broadland fens is the perennial marsh pea. It is scattered very locally indeed over Britain as a whole, and East Anglia is its stronghold, though it becomes remorselessly rarer even here. It has been recorded in some nine tetrads in the Broadland area and a handful of sites in West Norfolk and West Suffolk since 1970. It likes Broadland reedy fens, and may be viewed easily in fair quantity on the NWT Cockshoot Broad Reserve, as it scrambles to a metre or so in the reedbeds alongside the wooden walkway in June and July. If you do not wish to walk as far as the Broad, the marsh pea may also be seen growing on the NWT roadside reserve along the minor road from Woodbastwick down to the Bure, which gives access to Cockshoot. Other NWT sites are Burgh Common near Filby Broad, Ranworth Broad, and Upton Fen. It also grows in Norfolk on the Woodbastwick and Strumpshaw reserves. It was unrecorded from the Thurne Broads for many years, but was found beside Catfield Dyke at the west end of Hickling Broad in 1989. It grows locally in north-east Suffolk – near Outon Broad, Lowestoft, for instance, on the SWT Oulton Marshes – and there is an SWT west Suffolk site at Lakenheath Poors Fen. Floras describe its flowers uninspiringly as purplish-blue, but it is arguably the most attractive of the wild peas as the colour can in fact vary – partly with age – to include light blue and amethystine shades.

There are two white-flowered wetland umbellifers which also have East Anglia, and particularly the Broadland fens, as their stronghold. One is the bright green cowbane, which is very poisonous to cattle as its name suggests – though coypus were said to eat it with impunity. It was formerly abundant around broads and some fen ditches, but is now a local plant of our region and parts of central England, and is rare elsewhere. The second is the milk parsley, rare outside East Anglian fens though recorded since 1970 in 40 tetrads within the region. It is notable and crucial as the food-plant for swallowtail butterfly caterpillars. Both cowbane and milk parsley are absent from north-east Essex.

Petch and Swann tell us that Caldecote Fen in West Norfolk was blue with an abundance of the much-loved columbine in late springs and early summers before it was drained in 1959. There were even occasional purple and chocolate-brown flowers, and white and pink variants have also been recorded elsewhere. Flowers lingered on throughout the 1960s, but if you were allowed to visit Caldecote today, it may well be you would not be certain where the old fen was. The columbine is a native plant of woods, fens and calcareous grassland, preferring fen sedge-beds and thickets in East Anglia, but now more often than not the odd wayside flower one spots is a garden escape or throw-out, and the species occurs only as a casual in north-east Essex. Alec Bull has written of scattered plants and even stands in the hedgerows around Cranworth in central Norfolk when he came to live there in 1960, and columbines have been reported in wet woods on more acid soils south-east of King's Lynn as recently as 1994.

The affection in which the columbine is held is attested by its firm place in our gardens, but also by its tendency to attract local names, such as granny's bonnet, ladies' bonnets and – a delightful Suffolk coining – dollycaps. Its scientific binomial is *Aquilegia vulgaris*, *aquila* being the Latin for an eagle, which is supposedly suggested by the petal shape. 'Columbine', or course, makes the association with doves. If you look at the petal-spurs, strongly curved or even hooked at the end so as to resemble a dove's (or eagle's!) neck and head, and at the wing-like sepals, you will see the justice of the avian comparisons. But the similarity to an old-fashioned bonnet is equally apparent. Another East Anglian name is lady's shoes, and it was known as hens and chickens here and there in Norfolk. Columbines were regarded as lions' food in the Middle Ages, and one rubbed the plant in one's hands to acquire courage. The leaves were sometimes used as a poultice to reduce swellings, and other medicinal, allopathic and homeopathic applications of the columbine, often utilising the whole plant in flower to make an infusion, strain credulity in their variety: they include liver and gall bladder disorders, chronic skin irritations, menopausal ailments, scurvy, jaundice, nervous disorders and hysteria!

All is not lost as regards the survival of our native fenland columbine populations: the species reappeared in the early 1990s after many years' absence on the Norfolk Wildlife Trust Scarning Fen Reserve, near Dereham. Continued sympathetic management of other protected fens may yet induce futher resurrections.

One normally associates wintergreens with the woods and rock-ledges of Scotland and the north and not with lowland England, but the round-leaved wintergreen is an interesting exception which has been recorded in nutrient-poor areas of fens and in bogs and former turf-ponds in Norfolk, though it has declined dramatically in the county from its former presence in some 15 hectads to near-extinction, largely owing to the dwindling of turf and reed cutting. It stronghold remains north-central and north-eastern Scotland, however, with scatterings through northern England and a cluster of sites in Kent. The subspecies *maritima*, on the other hand (which has smaller leaves, flower-stalks and styles), grows almost exclusively in dune slacks or, at least, damp hollows on the Welsh coast and west coast of England.

Round-leaved wintergreen is a localized species in East Anglia: in Suffolk it is almost certainly extinct, and it has not been found in its former wet-heath sites since the last record

ABOVE: The late-summer marsh gentian, Buxton Hea[th] Norfolk. RIGHT: Marsh sowthistle, How Hill, Norfolk. At its [side] is the marshland form of the perennial sow thistle, someti[mes] mistaken for the rarer species. BELOW: Early marsh orc[hid] Thompson Common, Norfolk.

at Middleton in 1906. There are Essex records since 1970, though it has probably never been native in north-east Essex, and occurs only as an introduction. A good place to see it is the Essex Wildlife Trust Chigborough Lakes Reserve.

Round-leaved wintergreen is similar to many orchid species in relying on a symbiotic relationship with a mycorrhizal fungus partner to supply some of its nutrients for seedling growth and establishment, and it also shows some dependence in the mature phase. *Scarce Plants in Britain* points out its particular affinity with the fen orchid, as both plants, which once shared the same sites in Norfolk, have a declining eastern sub-species but a gradually increasing west coast race. The plant is an evergreen perennial whose sweetly-scented, nodding white flowers, which appear from July to September, are somewhat reminiscent of the lily-of-the-valley, but have a protruding, S-shaped style. The place to see it wild now is Upton Fen in Norfolk, though there is also a site at Winterton Dunes, which some East Anglian botanists have insisted is a rare east-coast occurrence of subspecies *maritima* despite outside assertions that it is only 'doubtfully reported' from eastern Britain. Subsp. *maritima* was also recorded as growing in the dunes at Wells, but was lost in the disastrous floods of 1953. All is not resolved by *Scarce Plants in Britain*, which shows both subspecies as extinct in the Wells 10km square, but records subsp. *rotundifolia* as present since 1970 in the Winterton Dunes hectad, whereas subsp. *maritima* is shown as lost there before that year.

Let us look now at some flowering plants of the ditches, ponds and rivers of East Anglia. Various species produce white flowers on, or held above, the surface of the water. The various water crowfoots usually have five petals and are thereby easily distinguished from the water-plantain and frogbit families with their three-petalled flowers. The water-plantains or fishleaves themselves carry whorls of small flowers above the surface, whilst arrowhead (sometimes called broad-arrow or serpent's-tongue in Broadland), has larger flowers with a purple spot and arrow-shaped, floating leaves. Frogbit has kidney-shaped, bronzy-green leaves (which prompted its local names penny-weed and halfpennies-and-pennies in pre-decimal currency days), and its white flowers have a yellow spot. The more interesting member of the frogbit family is the water-soldier, once known as pickerel-weed in Norfolk, which prefers calcareous water and is found in our region mainly in fen dykes, though it occurs also in ponds and, in times gone by, it choked parts of one or two broads. It is found more widely in East Anglia, especially Broadland, than elsewhere, though it has been widely introduced in other parts of the country and is firmly naturalised in some. Its range as a native has shrunk alarmingly, and there is now only a handful of such sites outside Broadland: in fact, it has been recorded as native in only seven tetrads since 1970 according to the latest national survey. In Suffolk, Lothingland was its stronghold: try SWT Carlton Marshes near Lowestoft and the dykes of the Castle Marshes near Beccles. Good Norfolk sites are the pools at Upton Fen and the dykes on Ludham Marshes and Burgh Common. The north-east Essex occurrences in ponds seem to have resulted from plantings.

Water soldier has, as its scientific name *Stratiotes aloides* suggests, aloe-like crowns of spine-toothed, light green leaves and these rise to the surface at flowering times in early summer. Then, allegedly weighed down by chalky deposits accumulated within the outer leaves, the plant sinks to the bottom again at the end of the season – possibly to protect itself from hard frosts – only to rise once more when the outermost leaves are shed in the following spring. An alternative theory has it that oxygen from vigorous spring and summer photosynthesis is stored in the leaves and stems, lending buoyancy, until diminishing activity in the autumn causes the sinking. There are only female plants native to Britain, though there were doubts until recently whether water soldier is a true native at all. The supply of flowers is often rather niggardly. But why 'soldier'? – *Stratiotes* is from the classical Greek for a soldier and is perhaps a reference to the saw-edged, soldierly, sword- or bayonet-like leaves of our plant and of other species of the genus.

Water soldier is often planted for ornamental purposes in garden pools and ponds, and one of the first convictions secured under the Wildlife and Countryside Act for removing a scheduled plant from the wild related to the unlawful collection of water soldier from Ludham Marshes.

The tall, conspicuous flowering rush, with its splendid, bright-pink umbels of flowers, has all too often been another victim of plant thieves, even though it is widely available from garden centres and waterplant nurseries. It often grows just out of arm's reach in the water of streams, rivers and ditches rather than at the side or on the saturated margin, but this is possibly because it is so often pillaged from sites with dry-feet accessibility, though the practice of river authorities cutting back vegetation on some stretches will not have helped it thrive. It is not now common. *Butomus*, from its scientific name *Butomus umbellatus*, comes from the Greek words *bous*, an ox, and *temno*, to cut (reflecting the fact that the sharp-edged leaves are unsuitable for fodder). It is the only species of its genus.

An early-summer glory of some of our ponds, ditches and slow-flowing rivers are the large colonies of water-violet, once known as water-gillofer, which can form sheets of pale lilac above the surface of the water. The flowers, in tiered whorls on the erect peduncles or stems, have yellow eyes, and the water-violet's membership of the primrose family seems less improbable when one examines them: they can be pin- or thrum-eyed. The stems float underwater and the yellow-green, finely-divided leaves are submerged. Lothingland is the area of Suffolk where the plant is most easily found: try Oulton Marshes. It is scarce elsewhere in the county. Only three sites – a ditch and two ponds – were found in the recent north-east Essex survey, and the plant is thus rare and decreasing there. One of the best Norfolk sites must be the pingos – those curious flocks of pools of glacial origin – at the NWT reserve at Thompson Common, though I have seen colonies in some stranger places, such as a tight-packed conifer plantation alongside the Norwich to Aylsham main road. Here, a brilliant oval of flowers filled a pool and lightened the arboreal gloom. Another delightful resident of the Thompson pingos is that large marsh buttercup, the scarce greater spearwort.

The bladderwort you are most likely to see in ditches and fen dykes, and which grew formerly in turf-pits in our region, is the common or greater bladderwort, *Utricularia vulgaris*. It bears pleasantly-bright, snapdragon-like yellow flowers on free-floating stems above feathery, submerged leaves, usually in base-rich still or very slow-moving water, though it does not invariably flower every year. It is more common in East Angloia than anywhere else in Britain, though it is now rare in Suffolk and seemingly extinct in north-east Essex. Try Ludham Marshes NNR or the Wildlife Trust reserves of Burgh Common or Roydon Common in Norfolk, and Sprats Water, Carlton Marshes in Suffolk. *Utricularia* is from the Latin *utriculus*, a small bottle, which refers to little bladders on the forked leaflets which trap insects and small water creatures.

A real East Anglian wetland speciality is the marsh sow-thistle. It is found as an undisputedly native perennial plant only in Norfolk and Suffolk, and Kent and the lower Thames, though the Hampshire plants not recorded until 1959 may well also be native. The marsh sow-thistle once grew further north in Lincolnshire and westwards as far as Leicestershire and Oxfordshire. As your boat passes it in fairly plentiful, sturdy ranks on the banks of the Ant or the Thurne in Norfolk, standing two or three yards high, you may doubt its rarity and, indeed, it has been claimed that it is as frequent now in Broadland as it was 250 years ago. One reason for its Norfolk resurgence this last half century in the teeth of national decline is said to be its liking for the dredgings taken from the rivers and deposited along their banks, though this does not seem to explain observations of its spreading in Suffolk southwards to marshes near the coast and estuaries, including those at Blythburgh, Minsmere, East Bridge, Snape, Tunstall and Iken. Possibly it also benefits from regular winter reed cutting. In Norfolk, you can see it at Horsey and along the Thurne at Thurne Village and Potter Heigham; along the Ant (How Hill gives good public riverside access to the plant); on the Bure at Acle and Stokesby; on the Surlingham to Reedham stretch of the Yare and along the Chet. In Suffolk, Lothingland is again the area to make for if you are close to the lower Waveney. In north-east Essex, it is present only as an introduction on the EWT Fingringhoe Nature reserve, where it is flourishing. It has also spread considerably through the Cambridgeshire fens from reintroductions.

As well as clayey river banks, the marsh sow-thistle likes reed beds, especially the marshy strips fringing the lower reaches of rivers known as reed-ronds. It prefers wet alluvial or peaty soils which are neutral to alkaline rather than acidic, and can put up with a degree of salinity along rivers affected by tides.

Much is made in some floras of the possibility of mistaking tall, marshland forms of the perennial or corn sow-thistle for the marsh sow-thistle, but in fact you will never confuse the two once you have seen the true marsh plant. The marsh sow-thistle is almost always significantly taller and more robust-looking, with smaller flowerheads of a paler yellow. If you are still unsure, look at the leaves: those of the corn sow-thistle are variably pinnately-lobed, but very rarely as deeply as the arrow-shaped lower ones (or as little as the upper ones) of the marsh sow-thistle.

The mires of East Anglian river valleys can, as we have seen, be alkaline and give rise to fen vegetation, but we are also quite well endowed with acid valley bogs where peat has accumulated in waterlogged conditions lacking oxygen, so that bacteria cannot thrive and break down the plant litter quickly and efficiently. Such valley bogs often occur alongside sandy heathland, which forms the adjacent, slightly higher terrain. The neophyte botanist may well be confused by the tendency of different ecologists to define mires differently: sometimes they are said to be adequately characterised as fens or bogs by their respective alkalinity or acidity; but sometimes bogs are said to be fed mainly by rainfall, whereas fens are usually base-rich mires fed by groundwater and surface run-off as well as rain. So, by these latter definitions, there are such rare things as base-poor fens!

We think of heaths as dry, fire-prone habitats, but the wetland situation is complicated even more by the existence of wet heath, a habitat intermediate between dry heath and bog. You can often see heathland passing quite suddenly to wet heath by, in fact, looking at the heaths (that is, the heathers) growing on them. Ignoring other plants characteristic of heathland such as gorse, broom and bracken, you will see, usually, pale purple ling or heather, perhaps with some rosy bell heather, growing in the dry heathland. But where the wet heath begins, the greyish cross-leaved heath, with clearer pink flowers, is likely to predominate.

Wet heath often has interesting plants such as petty whin, lousewort and heath spotted-orchid, but one beautiful rarity growing in East Anglia only in Norfolk must be savoured here. The marsh gentian is a very local perennial living up to two decades and found from Dorset and East Sussex to north-east Yorkshire and what was Cumberland. In Norfolk it has been recorded in only eight tetrads since 1970, and you are now likely to find it only at the NWT's East Winch Common and at Buxton Heath. It was reported to be 'hanging on in small numbers' at East Winch in 1993, and it is only a little more plentiful at Buxton Heath, growing where the dry heath shades into the wet. In Suffolk, it has not been seen since 1860. The plants vary greatly in size: up to 28 flowers on larger specimens have been recorded, as have pink and white flowers, but I think you will have to visit the stronghold of the species in the New Forest area to see such plants. The Norfolk plants usually have fewer blooms, with the typical colouring of a blue corolla with five green lines on the outside. Those in more open conditions generally flower more freely. Alone amongst the gentians of lowland England, they are of a really 'true blue' shade, though they are paler and far less brilliant than the wonderful upland spring gentians of Teesdale. Though *Gentiana pneumonanthe* is the source of a blue dye, photographers should beware: the blueness is very difficult to capture accurately on colour film. I tried blue filters, avoiding taking the pictures in sunshine, and photographed the flowers backlit, sidelit and frontlit, high and low – but not even the coldest, bluest light and the most blatant technological interventions produced transparencies which really satisfied me.

Gentians take their name from Gentius, Pirate King of Illyria, who used them medicinally, and indeed, *pneumonanthe* means 'lung flower' – because the species was thought to be efficacious in treating respiratory diseases. This name may have been suggested by the light spots on the inside of the petal-tube reminiscent of the spots on the leaves of lungwort, a plant credited with similar medicinal properties because the marked leaves resemble the lungs.

Buxton Heath, north-west of Norwich, is remarkable not only for its marsh gentians but also because you see four vegetation zones as acid heath shades through wet heath and then bog to alkaline fen. Some plants seem to tolerate both bog and fen conditions, or, in an unusual wetland site such as Buxton Heath, grow where the two zones merge. The delightful, procumbent pale-pink bog pimpernel is one such that I have seen at Buxton, though not for five or six years. It deserves its *Anagallis tenella* scientific appellation, as it certainly is dainty. *Anagallis* is from the Greek, meaning 'to laugh', because these plants were considered to dispel sadness. There is a wonderful garden form, *A. tenella* 'Studland'. It is a fairly common species in parts of the wet west, but is absent from much of the east of the country. It is now rare in Suffolk and scarce, I think, in Norfolk also, though you can still see it at Oulton Marshes, at the SWT North Cove Reserve near Barnby and at the NWT reserves of Booton Common near Reepham and Holt Lowes.

The sundews are fascinating plants also sometimes found on wet heaths as well as out-and-out acid bog. The common name is usually explained by reference to the way the stalked red, sticky glands glitter like dewdrops in the sunshine (sundews dislike shade) and the scientific generic *Drosera* is Greek for 'dewy'. But the name may be Anglo-Saxon 'sin-dew' or 'always dewy', and have no solar implication. The sticky glands trap insects to supplement the meagre nutritional fare available from the peaty soil.

There are, in fact, three sundews: the common or round-leaved, which is common in the north and west of Britain but absent from much of central, eastern and southern England; the oblong-leaved or long-leaved sundew, found mainly in the west; and the great sundew, with larger, longer leaves, which is much more local in distribution and is absent from much of England, Wales and eastern Scotland. Norfolk is the East Anglian county in which to search for sundews. In Suffolk, the oblong-leaved and great sundews are both almost certainly extinct, and Simpson reported that even the common sundew had almost disappeared from the county's wet heaths and bogs during the period of his survey in the 1970s, though you can still see it at Market Weston Fen. The common sundew – the only species recorded there – has long since disappeared from north-east Essex. In Norfolk, in the late 1960s, the common sundew was reported as locally abundant in bogs and wet heaths, the great sundew as much rarer in similar habitats and the oblong-leaved sundew as intermediate in frequency between the other two. The species are, in fact, fairly easily distinguished by leaf size and shape (though there are occasional hybrids), and the best place I know for a sundew hunt is Roydon Common in the north-west of the county. Despite the abundance of the common sundew at Roydon, you will do well to find even one with one of its small white flowers fully open. Also in Norfolk, great sundew grows at the NWT Scarning Fen, great and common sundew at Holt Lowes and Beeston Bog, and common sundew at Buxton Heath. The sundews have been used in proprietary medicines as expectorants to relieve whooping and other dry, persistent coughs, and the beads of 'dew', because they persist and defy evaporation by the sun, have caused the sundew to be considered traditionally a plant capable of transferring strength and endurance to human beings, preserving youth and functioning as an aphrodisiac.

Roydon is also known for its summer display of *Narthecium ossifragum*, the little bog asphodel, with its yellow tepals which eventually turn the colour of saffron and have indeed been used as a saffron substitute in the Northern Isles. The bog asphodel has also provided a hair dye. This is a common plant in bogs and other west, peaty, acid places on the heaths, moors and mountains of western and northern Britain, but it is not to be found across most of central and eastern England. In Norfolk, it grows only in the west of the county, Dersingham Bog being its only other surviving Norfolk station, and it was not recorded in Simpson's Suffolk survey, though he felt sure it once occurred on sites similar to those in west Norfolk. *Ossifragum* means 'bone-breaking' and came from a belief that sheep which ate the plant would develop brittle bones. This is probably groundless: such sheep as did succumb to fragile bones and broken limbs possibly literally fell victim to a more general nutrative deficiency in the vegetation of the poor, calcium-free land on which the bog asphodel grows. But, interestingly, an alleged case of suckling cows and their calves being poisoned so badly through eating the plant that 11 subsequently died from kidney damage has been reported recently from Ireland, and recent research does suggest the plant may inhibit the manufacture of vitamin D, vital to bone growth.

Another plant of bogs, wet heaths and even fens which, like the sundews, is partly insectivorous, is the dainty and innocuous-looking common butterwort. It has spurred violet flowers with a white patch in the throat which gives it the alternative common name of bog violet. Once more this is a plant rare in central and southern England, but locally common elsewhere. It is almost extinct in Suffolk, its home ground there being the fens of the Waveney Valley: try Thelnetham or Redgrave and Lopham Fens. In Norfolk, it is a little more widely findable: try Buxton Heath once more or the NWT reserves of Booton Common near Reepham, Scarning Fen near Dereham, or Holt Lowes.

'Butterwort' comes from the yellowish basal rosette of leaves and their greasy appearance, and the plant was said to protect milk and butter if cows' udders were rubbed with it. The edges of the leaves curl inwards to enfold the insect victims. As regards its scientific name, *Pinguicula vulgaris*, *Pinguis* is Latin for 'fat'. The plant overwinters as a bud at ground level.

Because it has such a beautiful flower, I must include the bogbean or buckbean despite its rather humdrum common names. It is ever harder to find in its characteristic habitats of bogs, fens, and shallow water at the edges of ponds, pools and ditches. The common names derive from the fact that its foliage is rather similar to that of a broad bean, though its ternate leaf – that is, a compound leaf comprising three leaflets – also gave it the local names of water trefoil and marsh clover in the 19th century. You can dry these leaves to make a tea which relieves migraine and headaches generally, or helps with poor appetite and digestion and stomach disorders, and they have also been used in place of hops in brewing. The roots were pounded prehistorically to produce flour, and also used to treat rheumatism, jaundice and the ague, so the bogbean certainly counts utility as well as beauty in its catalogue of attractions. If often forms dense mats, most plants of which do not flower, but those that do are welcome. I cannot do better than refer to the late Ted Ellis's description of the plant as bearing pink and white star flowers with petals faced and fringed with little white threads which glitter like spun glass, giving blossoms the beauty of frost crystals. It was called, more prosaically, white fluff in parts of Norfolk. Unfortunately, it is shallow-rooted and therefore likely to die out at sites which become drier. The bogbean is sometimes associated with the marsh cinquefoil, with its curiously attractive, prominent, dully wine-red sepals.

Finally, glances at two near-unique habitats. The Ouse Washes on Norfolk's western fringe comprise wet, neutral, lowland grassland: a long, fairly narrow strip of watermeadows subject to regular flooding in winter as part of the Great Ouse drainage and flood-relief system, which are used in the summer for grazing and hay. The ditches, like the Broadland dykes on the grazing marshes, are cleared out by dragline, and botanical diversity is thereby assured. The Washes are perhaps best known for their bird life, but over 260 plant species have been recorded, including narrow-leaved and water-dropwort and small water-pepper. So-called 'paramaritime' species such as the sea aster and the least lettuce have been found here some 20 miles inland, but the most attractive aquatic plant that seems particularly at home and plentiful here is the yellow-flowered fringed water-lily, which is actually a member of the bogbean family.

The Breckland meres always fascinate visitors, through they are not all of a kind. In some, the water level fluctuates hardly at all, but the interesting ones are those which fill from below as the water in the chalk gradually rises. Examples are Ringmere, Langmere, the Devil's Punchbowl and Fowlmere, all in the Wretham and Croxton area of the Norfolk Breck. The water level also falls after a drought, of course, but there can be considerable delays in both upward and downward movements, so the mere may be completely empty or the water level very low during an autumn and winter of heavy rainfall, but brimful or overflowing during a long summer dry spell. There are dead trees killed by previous inundations on the banks of some meres. It times gone by, crops were sometimes sown on the dry beds, but were occasionally lost to a rapid refilling of the mere. The recent succession of dry years had marked effects: Ringmere, for example, where six parishes meet on the NWT East Wretham Heath Reserve, hade dried out completely, with its bed almost bare of vegetation, by the summer of 1990. A series of fascinating plant communities succeeded, including a marginal ring of the unusual golden dock, which can also be seen at Cornard Mere near Sudbury and at the Essex Wildlife Trust's Chigborough Lakes, north of the Blackwater. At one stage in 1992, a mass of water chickweed covered the bed of Ringmere. The mere then remained dry even through the wetter summer and autumn of 1993 and into the winter of 1994, but by March it had refilled amply after the longest period without replenishment on record.

Other marginal plants of the Breckland meres include knotted pearlwort, celery-leaved buttercup and whorled mint.

LEFT: Common reed and yellow iris by the Thurne, Norfolk. RIGHT: Lady's-smock. BELOW: Yellow loosestrife.

LEFT: Ragged-robin. RIGHT: Yellow flag. BELOW: Yellow water-lily.

LEFT: Marsh helleborine. RIGHT: Meadow thistle. BELOW: Common valerian.

LEFT: Marsh fragrant orchid. RIGHT: Marsh thistle: white-flowered form. BELOW: Grass of Parnassus flowerhead. RIGHT: Round-leaved wintergreen.

ABOVE: Arrowhead. BELOW: Water-soldier and frogbit.

LEFT: Common bladderwort and frogbit. RIGHT: Bog pimpernel.
BELOW: Water violet.

Greater spearwort.

ABOVE LEFT: Common sundew. BELOW: Bog asphodel. ABOVE RIGHT: Butterwort. BELOW: Bogbean.

ABOVE: Bed of Ringmere covered in water chickweed in October, 1992. INSET: Ringmere dry in October 1990. TOP: Marsh cinquefoil.

LEFT: Jersey cudweed. RIGHT: Sea aster.

BESIDE THE SEA

> ... half way down
> Hangs one that gathers sampire, dreadful trade!
> William Shakespeare, *King Lear*

It is no surprise that the diverse East Anglian coastline, rich in interest for geologist and ornithologist alike, should be blessed also with a fascinating range of wild flowers. Our coast may not boast the craggy cliffs and rocky coves of some parts of the western seaboard, but there is terrain varied enough to provide a wide range of wildflower habitats from the drowned river estuaries of north-east Essex and south-east Suffolk to Hunstanton's tri-coloured chalk and limestone cliffs, where the wild wallflower clings, just a little less giddily, perhaps, than would the 'sampire' on Shakespeare's more lofty cliff in Kent.

If the estuaries are included in the calculation, there is well over 300 miles of coastline bordering our region, though man's activities have of course ensured that not all of it is available now for wildflower species characteristic of coastal habitats. North-east Essex, threatened by rising sea levels, is the area most transformed, with the old middle and upper saltmarshes cut off from the sea by protecting sea walls along most of the coastline. This shielded land, once grazing marshes, is now more often than not appropriated for urban, industrial or leisure development or made over to arable farming: it is estimated that some 80% of reclaimed saltmarsh grassland has been lost over the past half-century. There is also very little surviving natural sand and shingle beach, though some dunes remain at Colne Point, Dovercourt, Crabknowe Spit, Stone Point, Mersea and Bradwell-on-Sea. There are low, London Clay cliffs at Clacton and in the Frinton area, but only Walton has true cliffs, which comprise red crag. Features of the north-east Essex coast are the shellbanks to be found at Colne Point, Walton, Dovercourt and on the edge of the Dengie Marshes. Wildlife protection is afforded by the National Nature Reserves at Hamford Water, the Colne Estuary and the Blackwater Estuary, and by several Essex Wildlife Trust coastal reserves.

The river estuaries and muddy creeks continue in south-east Suffolk, and good saltmarsh habitats remain along the south side of the Blyth from Blythburgh to Walberswick, along the Alde at Snape Warren, north of the Ore at Shingle Street, and on the north bank of the Deben: about a third of Suffolk's saltmarshes are in the Deben estuary, in fact. But the wash of ships and possibly also channel dredging and the rise in sea-level have caused much erosion of the saltings on both sides of the Orwell and towards the mouth of the Stour estuary.

Soft, low cliffs of various glacial clays, sands, shelly crags and pebble beds are a feature of the Suffolk coast, most notably between Bawdsey Haven and East Lane; between Sizewell, Minsmere and Dunwich; from Southwold to Covehithe; at Pakefield and Gunton and between Hopton, Corton and Gorleston. The sand and shingle beaches derive mostly from cliff erosion, though significant systems of marram dunes are found only between Sizewell and Dunwich, and Suffolk dunes are mainly acidic. Splendidly extensive pebble beaches, ridges and spits hosting and fronting interesting communities of maritime plants occur from Shingle Street to Bawdsey East Lane and from the mouth of the Ore to Orford Ness and Aldeburgh, and a shingle beach stretches from Dunwich Gap to Walberswick. Sand and shingle beaches are to be found at Felixstowe Ferry and Bawdsey, between Aldeburgh and Sizewell, at Dunwich, Easton Bavents, Covehithe and Benacre Ness, and at the Lowestoft North and South Denes. Though some stretches of the Suffolk seaboard are like the Essex coast in that they have been modified or appropriated for human purposes (particularly from Kessingland north into Norfolk), yet Suffolk retains more extensive and varied wildflower habitats than north-east Essex and enjoys many protected sites such as the stretches of 'Heritage Coast' and the nature reserves: Dunwich, Benacre National Nature Reserve, the parts of Orfordness in the care of the National Trust and English Nature, Walberswick and Havergate Island NNR's, Minsmere, Boyton Marshes and the rump of Landguard Common (the very southernmost tip of the county), are examples. Almost the entire Suffolk coastline comprises sites designated Sites of Special Scientific Interest or County Wildlife Sites.

The tourist industry pressurises but does not always obliterate coastal wildflower habitats. In Norfolk the North Denes at Great Yarmouth, where sea-holly and sheepsbit remain quite plentifully among the litter, is an example, and the unspoilt National Nature Reserve of Winterton Dunes lies not far to the north. Thence runs the often slender barrier of dunes between the sea and the broads and marshes, finally giving way to 21 miles of crumbling, land-slipping cliffs of glacial deposits from south of Happisburgh to Cromer and beyond. Finally, and most fruitfully for wild flowers, there stretches the long series of sandflats, shingle ridges and marshes from Weybourne west to the Wash, including the greatest saltmarsh system in eastern England.

The relative wildness of the Norfolk seaboard, particularly the protected north coast – a 25 mile chain of nature reserves inviolate and unbroken except narrowly at Wells – of course suits most of its plants as much as its birds and other wildlife. Man has modified stretches of the county's coastline through building works, the construction of sea defences, and agricultural practices such as marsh drainage, but Norfolk is fortunate in retaining a good mileage of that narrow, primeval strand where sea interacts with shore much as it always has. Here are the habitats to which characteristically coastal plants are adapted and where they may still sometimes be found in abundance.

A number of plants play a vital part in the creation of saltmarshes and dunes and in stabilising shingle. Many of these have inconspicuous flowers or are grasses, such as marram, lyme, sand and sea couch, and the cord-grasses. Though these have their interest, it seems best here to concentrate largely on the showier flowering plants that more obviously gladden the eye and the heart of the coastal stroller. So, for instance, though such inconspicuous flowerers as the various oraches and the prickly saltwort (something of a menace to the barefoot holidaymaker) may grow immediately above the high tide mark, also to be seen is that attractive mauve crucifer, the sea rocket, an opportunistic plant often rooted improbably in pure sand within easy reach of the first angry high tide of autumn. But it is an annual which in fact can employ the sea as a dispersal agent to cast up its seeds elsewhere and ensure its continuance as a species, though the individual plants must perish each year. It is not universally abundant on our sandy beaches, but is best described as locally frequent, sometimes in colonies, though it does better in some seasons than others.

Like cacti, both the saltwort and the rocket have succulent leaves, as do many other maritime plants, in order to store water, endure the burning sands of summer and lose little moisture in the salty environment. Even the driftline oraches are not uniformly dull: the tolerably common frosted orache, sometimes called the mealy orache, possesses diamond-shaped leaves which are silvered as if covered by tiny sugar crystals. The less attractive but more scarce long-stalked orache is to be found on the Norfolk side of the Wash.

Higher up the sandy beach – but often very little higher – where the youngest dunes are forming, grows one of my favourite seaside plants. The sea-holly, a handsome thing when growing lustily bears spiny, blue-grey leaves with white veins and margins: like holly in shape but not in colour. The egg-shaped flowers, in what botanists call 'tight umbels', develop to a delicate powder blue and attract insects in profusion – most winningly when they include colour-coordinated common blue butterflies. The sea-holly also sprouts considerable folklore and bears a host of other human connections. Its long roots (up to two metres!) were once candied with sugar and orange-flower water: there were 'Eryngo-diggers' in Great Yarmouth in the 17th century (its scientific name is *Eryngium maritimum*), and the plant is mentioned in 1597 in Gerard's *Herbal*. The roots were boiled until they could be peeled, then thinly sliced and cooked again with an equal weight of sugar. They were then removed from the resultant syrup and allowed to cool. It is claimed that the candying was invented or first practised in Colchester even earlier, in the 15th century, and that the candied roots were still being made to the original recipe and sold in the streets of the town at least up to the end of the 19th century. The sea-holly is allegedly an aphrodisiac and, much less romantically, relieves flatulence. It 'makes goats stand still' and prevents lovers straying, which the coarse-minded may fancy to be two ways of describing one effect. Falstaff mentions the plant in *The Merry Wives of Windsor*. Unfortunately, it has been much uprooted by gardeners near the popular resorts, but there remain good displays of it here and there: near Gun Hill, Burnham Overy Staithe, in Norfolk and – more abundantly – at Thorpeness in Suffolk, for example. The EWT Colne Point reserve is a good north-east Essex site, where you can also see yellow horned-poppy, shrubby seablite and sea heath.

Also flowering on the newer 'yellow dunes' at Gun Hill from midsummer onwards is the pretty sea bindweed or sea convolvulus, which seems to be less common in Suffolk and was recorded recently as having four north-east Essex sites, including Colne Point. In flower size, sea bindweed sometimes falls not a great deal short of the large, white hedge bindweed one sees a little further inland, but it is striped pink and white, rather like a glamorous version of some colour forms of the smaller field bindweed. Its flowers close at night. The sea spurge is another plant of sandy sites.

Sand dunes appear an inhospitable habitat, but in fact the hills and hollows of the older-established 'grey dunes' may support a rich and varied flora, especially where the 'lows' are eroded down to the water table and become 'dune slacks' carrying water in the wetter seasons. Unfortunately, East Anglian dunes are not richly endowed with slacks. Dune systems in general seem arid places in the heat of summer, but often have a layer of fresh water within them, above the salt water from the sea. The shell fragments in the sand of many new dunes create a growing medium favoured by lime-loving species, while in older dunes the calcium carbonate may be leached from the upper layer of sand. They become covered with lichens, mosses, grasses and sand sedge and, in time, a thin, spongy, water-holding layer of peat may form from these in some of the hollows, so that acid-loving bog and heath plants appear.

Many flowers found on established dunes also grow in sandy or waste places inland: bright yellow ragwort and even fireweed (rosebay willowherb) among the taller kinds; pink – or occasionally white – storksbill, the biting and English stonecrops, yellow lady's bedstraw, catsear and the delicately-perfumed, bright pink centaury among the shorter. The last of these has aristocratic connections, being of the gentian family – and its breeding shows. This annual, the delicately-perfumed blooms of which close at night, sometimes appears in a white-flowered form, as on Pakefield cliffs in Suffolk. It has been used as a tonic in convalescence, but, despite its alternative common name of feverwort, its efficacy as a febrifuge is said to be very limited. A small Norfolk colony of the scarcer small or lesser centaury was recorded at Holme in 1994; a plant I recall seeing at Cley some years ago.

At Holkham, in north Norfolk, lime-loving ploughman's spikenard and the withered-looking carline thistle grow, but on the very acid older dunes of Winterton to the south-east, there is the remarkable sight of our three more common heathers growing in close proximity: abounding, lilac-purple ling, rosy bell heather and, in damper areas, the clear, pale pink spikes of cross-leaved heath.

Though monomaniacal wildflower twitchers akin to the ornithological kind are mercifully few, it cannot be denied that aficionados do love to see the odd rarity, and Norfolk dunes hold one or two of these. The Jersey cudweed is an annual covered in white, woolly hairs and bears small yellow florets. As its name indicates, it is native to the Channel Islands and was probably introduced to all remaining British mainland sites, save its Norfolk station. It is unexciting in everything except its extreme rarity. Even in Norfolk, though between 50 and 60 plants were recorded in the mid-sixties, it disappeared until rediscovered 'in quantity' in 1978. Do not expect to find masses of the cudweed amid north Norfolk dunes at present as there have been few plants in flower in recent years. The conservation body responsible for the site has made efforts to maintain the wet habitat the species and the accompanying natterjack toads require, and has raised plants on site. I remember one magical summer's day, while standing stock-still watching natterjack toadlets, seeing a stoat appear upwind of the site. It approached me with untroubled self-assurance and, obviously oblivious of my ample presence, all but trotted over my foot as it proceeded about its business. Such are the bonuses, sometimes, of solitary botanising.

In addition to the dunes, north Norfolk has its shingle banks and spits, most dramatically at Scolt Head Island, a Norfolk Wildlife Trust and National Nature reserve, and at Blakeney Point, in the care of the National Trust. In fact, the dune systems here also rest on old shingle foundations. Banks of mobile shingle may seem even less suitable wildflower habitats than dunes, and, in truth, little does grow on the wave-shuffled, weather-beaten seaward side of such banks as are next to the sea. But on the more sheltered leeward side and on the crests themselves, many colourful flowers with deep-searching root systems are anchored and draw on the surprisingly sufficient supplies of water held within the banks. Sometimes, both in Norfolk and further south along the East Anglian coastline, there is a series of storm ridges with troughs between, in which cases the fine shingle on the ridges tends to bear most vegetation rather than the coarser pebbles of the troughs. In time, decaying material from the plants that pioneer colonisation of the shingle forms humus, facilitating occupation by further species unable to grow in pure shingle. Where there are a number of banks and troughs behind the ridge closest to the sea, acid heath in the shape of a thin crust of turf providing a habitat for yet more plants may become established.

Look in early summer for the white cushions of sea campion (an excellent shingle stabiliser), the taller sea-beet, and, a little later, the showy yellow horned-poppy with its crinkled, silver-haired leaves and large yellow flowers, each of which opens and withers in a day. The long seed-pods are the 'horns'. Occasionally the poppy grows just a little inland.

On Suffolk shingle beaches, and sometimes on those where sand and pebbles are mixed, grows a real speciality of the county. The handsome sea pea appears, often abundantly, in all suitable habitats between Landguard and Kessingland and seems, in fact, to have been increasing in recent years. Paradoxically, it is more common here at the edge of its range than anywhere else in western Europe, yet it is probably not a Norfolk native and was recorded recently in north-east Essex nowhere other than on the dunes just south of Dovercourt. The sea or beach pea does not climb or scramble upwards like most peas, but tends to form thick, almost prostrate mats, above which it holds its red-purple flowers, fading to blue, and also its pods even quite early in the season. In years gone by, during times of acute food shortage, poor coast dwellers were known sometimes to eat the seeds of the sea pea. The claim is often repeated – one suspects by those who have never tried them – that they taste not unlike garden peas. Eskimos allegedly use them as a kind of coffee bean equivalent. You may admire the species in Norfolk at Cley, where seeds were sown by the late Ted Ellis in the 1950s. Walk along the shingle in the direction of Blakeney Point from the Norfolk Wildlife Trust's car park until you find patches of the characteristically yellowish leaves of the sea sandworth. There you should also find three or four patches of sea pea, which, thankfully, have survived the disastrous sea breakthrough of February 1996 (which flooded the NWT reserve at Cley) and the consequent radical disturbances of the shingle. Elsewhere on the north Norfolk coast, in damp hollows of the dunes at Holkham, another pea, *Lathyrus heterophyllus*, has grown since 1949. It seems to be naturalised nowhere else in Britain, and so has been christened the Norfolk everlasting pea.

My favourite Suffolk site for sea pea is just south of the village at Shingle Street, where a white-flowered form was once found, but there is also lots of it easily accessible at the SWT Thorpe Haven reserve, or alternatively between Kessingland Beach and Benacre Ness, with wild carrot and the occasional plant of sea kale. This last is a good site for seaside plants generally, even before one enters the National Nature Reserve at Benacre Sluice, with lots of tree lupin bearing flowers of pale yellow, or sometimes white tinged violet or purple – a Californian species so widely and firmly naturalised that Kessingland has been called 'Lupin Land'. There is also sheepsbit and rest-harrow at the rear of the beach and even the odd (non-native) plant of the rare white mullein to be found. The sweet roots of rest-harrow have been eaten instead of liquorice. Be circumspect if you take the walk further south to Benacre Broad, not only on account of the eroding coastline, but also because of the little tern nesting colony between the broad and the sea. Just south of Benacre Sluice there are some patches of the sea milkwort, or black saltwort, a small-flowered but attractive member of the primrose family. In our region it grows on the grassy margins of saltmarshes, muddy hollows in the saltings, or the banks of the lower reaches of Broadland rivers which are regularly tide-washed, though I have seen it in the Hebrides preferring quite shady niches between large seashore rocks.

The sea pea can also be found, in small quantity, on the beach beneath Pakefield Cliffs. The cliffs themselves are well worth exploring, for the rare-ish yellow vetch has been recorded here and at Shingle Street. In Suffolk, it prefers shingle beaches, but is occasionally found on sandy beaches and cliffs, and can be very locally abundant. It has been recorded since 1970 as native in 10 east Suffolk tetrads. In Norfolk I have seen it only at an inland roadside verge site at Briston as an introduced plant and Petch and Swann were adamant that it is merely an established alien in the county. It did once grow similarly as an introduced species in north-east Essex, but has not been seen in recent years. Also on less coarsely-vegetated stretches of Pakefield Cliffs to the south of the caravan park you may spot light-blue flowers of pale or narrow-leaved flax, now very rare in East Anglia, among the pink and white flowers of the centaury. It was quite plentiful when I visited Pakefield in high summer, 1994. Do not confine yourself to the clifftop path, which gives only intermittent views of the grassy cliff-slopes and too often tunnels through thick scrub, but walk along the beach, scanning the low cliffs from beneath.

Amongst the plentiful sea pea and sea poppy at Shingle Street, or perhaps even closer to the high tide mark, you may see the occasional plant of the long-lived sea kale in solitary magnificence. It usually grows in small colonies or as a single specimen on sites subject to erosion, though there are one or two reasonably-sized colonies in Suffolk and a magnificent host of plants thrive towards the north end of the SWT nature reserve at Landguard Point. This Suffolk colony may have imperialistic ambitions, for Tarpey and Heath speculate that the increasing numbers of sea kale sites being found across on the north-east Essex coast south of Harwich could result from colonising seed being swept from Landguard because of a modified tidal flow caused by the deep dredging operations necessitated by the development of Felixstowe Dock. No sites at all were recorded in this part of Essex before 1862; now there are at least six. The plant can also reproduce from broken-off roots. Another north-east Essex site is the EWT Bradwell Shell Bank Reserve.

The story in Norfolk on the other hand is less triumphant. Petch and Swann described sea kale in 1968 as very rare, though once abundant in the county, and the *Atlas of British Flora* showed no Norfolk records after 1930, though *Scarce Plants in Britain* does give post-1970 records on the east side of the Wash – try the shingle bank at Snettisham – and on the north Norfolk coast. Seed was introduced at Cley in 1912 and plants have survived there: I saw one in robust but solitary health as I took a walk along the shingle towards the old Watch House on Blakeney Point after viewing the sea pea in the late summer of 1993. Like sea pea, sea kale may be eaten as a vegetable and is doubtless more palatable: on the south coast near Beaulieu in the New Forest, the Montagu family once protected the plants on their foreshore so the crinkly leaves might regularly find their way to their stately kitchen. Less aristocratic coast-dwellers in our region used to heap shingle on the new, growing shoots to blanch them and remove any bitterness. The shoots and lower parts of the leaf stalks can be boiled in salted water for about 20 minutes and served in melted butter, lemon juice or sauce hollandaise, or, alternatively, boiled for 10 minutes before being sautéed in butter or olive oil until tender. Leaves can be boiled, then minced and seasoned with a couple of cloves of garlic and served as spinach, and young shoots and leaves of sea kale have also been used for salads, but we are not dealing here with a plant of the abundance of marsh samphire, and I have always resisted picking from it.

If you visit Landguard to see the sea kale, be sure also to pause at the fenced compound where conditions favourable to the growth of the now very rare stinking goosefoot are maintained. Spotting the small, inglorious plants from the fence is a challenge, but the SWT warden will assist when he comes by. It is a species fully justifying its name, as brushing it with the fingers ensures they will smell of rotten fish for an hour or two afterwards, deriving from the insect-attracting Trimethylamine present in the plant. It now has only three British stations.

While on the subject of rarities, the hog's fennel, or sulphurweed, should be mentioned. This robust umbellifer with yellow flowers grows as an undisputedly native plant only at Faversham in Kent and in rough grassland around Hamford Water (of Arthur Ransome's *Secret Water* fame) in north-east Essex, though not at its original Naze site. The Hamford Water sites include the Essex Wildlife Trust's Skipper's Island reserve. The caterpillar of

Fisher's estuarine moth, found in Britain only around Hamford Water, feeds on the stem of hog's fennel, which plant is quite common on the sea walls and islands and even occurs sometimes on the roadsides: it is ironic that some of the more accessible stands of sulphurweed are threatened by people seeking out the moth! Also to be seen growing on sea walls are the knotted hedge-parsley and the slender thistle.

South-east Suffolk and north-east Essex boast, in fact, a notable collection of scarce maritime and sub-maritime plants. Also from the *umbelliferae*, like hog's fennel, is slender hare's-ear, which is found on the dry, brackish grassland of sea walls and drained grazing marshes. Dittander is a scarce crucifer, which has this area as its British heartland and sometimes also grows on sea walls and very occasionally in saltmarshes, but in our region is most plentiful on the sides of rivers, creeks, ditches and in the brackish upper estuarine marshes near Colchester and Ipswich. The species can also be found in north-east Essex on waste places inland. It once had a culinary use as an alternative to horseradish.

Look out also in south-east Suffolk and north-east Essex for scarce clovers. Clustered cover and bird's-foot clover both grow predominantly near the sea, the former on sandy, dry soils, the latter in barish places in coastal turf. The sea clover has a range of habitats – grassy sea walls, brackish meadows, along tidal rivers and creeks and on the edge of saltmarshes and saltings – but is more or less limited in north-east Essex to the sea walls and grassy stretch between the wall and borrow dyke. The suffocated clover, also to be found near the sea, was once also an inland species, but remains so in Britain with any conviction only in the Suffolk Breck. It occurs along the Suffolk coast and into south-east Norfolk, but has not been recorded recently in north-east Essex.

The most striking summer display of East Anglian coastal flowers is to be found on the saltmarshes in the form of a lilac haze of great lawns of common sea-lavender, like heather moors or heaths. Norfolk is particularly well blessed on its north coast, where saltmarshes have developed widely behind sand bars, spits and even, here and there, on the open coast – anywhere where the currents were not too swift, and the tides were slight, fine mud or silt brought in by the sea could be deposited on the sandflats. The mudflats rose and wide channels gave way to winding creeks as more deposits collected and progressively less tidal water reached the upper levels of the marsh. The process has of course also occurred extensively elsewhere on the East Anglian coastline, and the relatively sheltered estuaries of south-east Suffolk and north-east Essex provided good conditions for saltmarsh development, though changing currents and the sinking of the coastline (some four metres in Essex since Roman times) can work against saltmarsh formation. Saltmarshes, together with shingle ridges, represent the most 'natural' climax habitats of our region, and the marshes are naturally zoned, with different plant species growing at different levels of the tidal range.

Plants assist considerably in building the saltmarshes. The best-known coloniser of the bare mud, helping create the lower marsh (whose seaward verge is usually close to the level of high neap tides), is glasswort, the so-called marsh samphire. This is a fleshy, succulent plant with shiny, segmented stems designed for water storage, which is still occasionally gathered in August to be boiled as a vegetable (it comes from the spinach family) and eaten with butter or pepper and vinegar, or pickled. Young shoots are sometimes picked in June or July and eaten raw in salads. If you pick a shoot from the saltmarsh and nibble it, you will find it merely salty and pleasantly crunchy, and not characterised by the strong spinach taste that some allege. But avoid polluted shorelines. Marsh samphire is sold on some Norfolk markets, and, indeed, appears increasingly on the menus of the more adventurous regional and metropolitan restaurants. Glasswort was once also dried and burnt, as was seaweed in Scotland, to produce the alkaline soda-ash for use in glassmaking and also in the manufacture of soap and linen. This useful but normally unspectacular plant comes into its own in the late summer and autumn, when the different forms can produce carpets of shades of red on the unprepossessing mud.

In Norfolk, the various kinds of glasswort are simply called 'samphire' because the true samphire is not found in the county and so does not need to be distinguished from glasswort. Confusion can easily arise elsewhere, for the unrelated rock samphire, the 'herbe de *Sainte Pierre*', is a spicily aromatic plant which also can be pickled in vinegar or brine, or its leaves and stalks boiled in water for about 10 minutes and eaten like asparagus in melted butter. The plant, claimed to be good for the heart, was once also an ingredient in a sauce used to garnish meat dishes. It occurs rarely in Suffolk, having been seen at Felixstowe, Shingle Street, Walberswick and further north at Kessingland and Pakefield, and equally rarely at three sites in north-east Essex, including Colne Point and Great Oakley. It will cling to high cliffs elsewhere in the country, though this has not made it secure from picking in the past: it is the plant Shakespeare refers to in *King Lear* as posing a 'dreadful' danger to those who gather it. It also grows less challengingly on rocks and, in our region, on old shingle beaches.

Rock samphire is a greyish umbellifer with yellow flowers bright with nectar, which can hardly be confused visually with the minute-flowered glasswort, but a third 'samphire' provides further cause for confusion. This is golden samphire, a member of the daisy family with rayed yellow flowerheads and similar leaves to rock samphire, which may be found on coastal cliffs and shingle elsewhere, but usually occurs in our region on sandy bars in saltmarshes, and on the upper saltings. It is a Mediterranean species that just used to make it in small numbers as far north as Shotley and Trimley in Suffolk, but still occurs in some quantity in Essex at Stansgate on the Blackwater, and at the Essex Wildlife Trust reserves of Howlands Marsh near St Osyth and Ray Island, though it has gone from the Stour.

At a slightly higher level of the saltmarsh than the annual glasswort, the sea aster grows. It can have pale purple rays (what most of us would call petals) radiating from the golden centre of disc-florets, creating a wild seaside equivalent to garden drifts of small Michaelmas daisies. Unfortunately, a drab form of the sea aster, totally lacking the rays, prevails over large areas of our region in place of the rayed kind.

The common sea-lavender, which produces such magnificent carpets of colour in our summer salt marshes, appealed so much to the Elizabethans that they grew it in their gardens after incorporating crushed rock-salt with the soil. It is a mid-marsh plant, as is sea purslane, which is dusted with small golden flowers but is more notable for the silver-greyness of the rest of the plant. It is often mixed in with the sea-lavender, but a favourite haunt is the sides of creeks. It is particularly effective in marsh-building, as it sieves out and holds mud wafted through it by the tides. The fleshy leaves, coated with diminutive scales to minimize water loss, can be used in salads or stir-fried with fish or meat. Other flowers such as the white-flowered common scurvy-grass and the pink or white greater sea spurrey also occur in the marsh. One species of scurvy-grass, *Cochlearia anglica*, also grows on islands far north in the Arctic and, so it is said, was picked by mariners in days gone by and eaten to ward off scurvy, being rich in Vitamin C. However, all the scurvy-grasses are said to share this characteristic, and another version has it that plants were gathered locally and taken on board ship before a long voyage, as they 'travel well'. Scurvy-grass sandwiches and drinks were consumed also by British landlubbers as anti-scorbutics well into the 19th century and leaves were collected after the plant had flowered to be added to various soups and sauces.

Perhaps the most fascinating area to those with an eye for wild flowers is the drier fringe of the high marsh. It is always pleasing to find the silvery foliage of the sea wormwood or sea southernwood here (though it also grows on the cliffs at Clacton), for it is one of our most aromatic plants, though some find its scent too pungent. Its woolly down conserves moisture. Put dried sprigs of sea wormwood in your wardrobe to deter moths. Where shingle has become compacted with sand, one may find the lesser sea spurrey and the rock sea-lavender, which is smaller and more delicate than its robust relation of the lower marsh. Sometimes the two species of sea-lavender do intermingle, but the rock sea-lavender is much rarer in Norfolk (try the 'laterals' on Blakeney Point) and very rare in the rest of our region, with a couple of sites in Suffolk and two or three in north-east Essex. Sea-lavenders belong to the genus *Limonium*, taken from the Greek *limne*, a marsh, or possibly from *leimon*, a meadow. On the western seaboard, you would find the rock sea-lavender's amethystine flowers, with persistent papery bracts around them, mainly on rocky cliffs, hence its name.

Best of all on the drier fringes is the deep-rooted sea pink, or thrift, when it grows in the mass exuding its delectable honey scent from flowers which may come in any shade of pink and even, rarely, in white. The 'plant of sympathy', as it is sometimes known, is allegedly called thrift because its leaves are evergreen (and possibly also because the flowers are followed by pleasing 'everlasting' papery seed heads), so that it thrives all year long. However, this is not always true of the leaves in extremely exposed situations.

The saltmarsh fringe habitat is most notable in East Anglia as the home of three plants at or very near their geographical limit in north Norfolk. Matted sea-lavender (the smallest of the family, wiry and many-branched almost like a bonsai-ed flowering tree, as the basal rosettes of daisy-like leaves die by flowering time) and sea-heath (a mat-forming species with narrow leaves like a diminutive heather) are both Mediterranean plants. Matted sea-lavender is found in Britain now only in Norfolk, where it continues to thrive. It grows in North Norfolk, and was found formerly in Lincolnshire, close to the Wash, but it is absent from north-east Essex and there are only old, vague, disputed records in Suffolk. Sea-heath is a native plant only as far north as Lincolnshire, though it is found outside our region also here and there on the southern English coast. It seems to be limited now to its Colne Point site in north-east Essex and is also very rare in Suffolk, though it has been found in salt marshes beside the Ore and at Hollesley, Blythburgh and Walberswick: a definite site is the SWT Simpson's Saltings Reserve near Hollesely, where sea kale and sea pea also grow. The sea-heath is a little more easily found in north Norfolk: a walk from Burnham Overy Staithe to Gun Hill may be crowned by finding the plant and matted sea-lavender growing almost intermingled.

The third of the trio is at the much larger shrubby seablite, in both colour and appeal at rather dull evergreen shrub of a little more than a metre in height, which also manages to struggle as far north only as Lincolnshire. Though you can find it scattered elsewhere in southern England – on Chesil Beach in Dorset, for example – its British heartland is Essex, and there are huge populations on Osea Island, Mersea Island and at Colne Point. It is not terribly difficult to find in north Norfolk – try the rear of the shingle ridge between Cley and Blakeney Point, or the beach at Holkham Gap – yet Simpson records it as very rare in Suffolk, with a single bush hanging on at Trimley in the 1980s. The shrubby seablite has the ability to survive being buried and of pushing up again through the sea-heaped shingle,

LEFT: Purple broomrape at a north-east Norfolk clifftop site. RIGHT: Sea pea: a Suffolk speciality in flower and fruit at Shingle Street in June. BELOW: Autumn marsh samphire turning red in front of the Old Lifeboat House, Blakeney Point, Norfolk. RIGHT: Sea bindweed on the dunes at Gun Hill, Norfolk.

though you may think it defies the botanical books by growing in sand rather than compacted shingle at Holkham Gap. However, the sand here overlies pebbles only thinly.

I must find room here for another favourite plant that grows near the sea, though admittedly it can grow besides brackish ditches (often in grazing marshes a little way inland converted to arable – it dislikes being grazed or cut), as well as on the extreme upper edges of the saltmarshes. The marsh mallow is a prominent plant with large flowers of rose pink (or sometimes a slightly paler shade than that), and light grey-green leaves. It is by no means common now, though it can be locally plentiful where it does occur, and has been recorded in over a dozen tetrads in our region since 1970. Good sites are the edge of the Snape Saltings Nature Reserve in Suffolk and, in small quantity, along the Stour in Essex from Copperas Wood to Manningtree – in both cases, where trees meet the grassy upper edge of the saltmarsh. It reaches its north European limit on the north shore of the Wash. A rather tangled thread is encountered when one tries to unravel the origins of 'mallow', which seemingly has come to us from Anglo-Saxon *malwe* and the Latin *malva*, both deriving from the Greek *malache*. This in turn came from another Greek word, *malakos*, meaning soft, because it is an emollient. This fits nicely with the scientific name, *Althaea officinalis*: the generic *Althaea* is from other Greek words – *althaia* (healing medium) and *althaine* (to heal) – and the specific, *officinalis* (of the shop), confirms the long use of the marsh mallow for medicinal purposes. The powdered root, mixed with cold water, has been used, to rather limited effect, in treating coughs in children and old people and as a gargle or mouthwash. The leaves can be used in a herbal compress on minor burns and cuts slow to heal. It is, of course, rather better known for the gluey confection originally made from its white, soft, moist, viscous roots, which herbalists also used to make a soothing jelly, and there was a strong east-coast tradition of gathering the plant.

The frequently unstable cliffs along parts of the East Anglian coastline are often of rather more interest to the geologist than the botanist, though the Pakefield Cliffs have been noted as an exception. However, where the clifftops are grassy and the farmer has judiciously kept his plough a yard or two from the crumbling edge, a pleasing variety of wild flowers may grow, though these are rarely uniquely maritime species. Some plants also found inland may also appear in unusual profusion here: the rest-harrow, for instance, the matted roots of which impeded the plough or the harrow in days when only truly equine horse-power was available for agricultural work. This plant, once known as rassals in Suffolk and land-whin more generally in East Anglia, taints milk, butter and cheese if cows graze it. The bird's-foot trefoil, known as 'bacon and eggs' because some of the bright yellow flowers may be streaked red, also does particularly well close to the sea. Its pods end in a curious claw, which probably accounts for its old Suffolk names of crowfeet and pig's-foot, and fingers-and-toes or five fingers in Norfolk, Essex and Cambridgeshire. It is the food-plant of the common blue caterpillar.

Let us end our wildflower tour of the coast with a great rarity of Norfolk clifftops between Sheringham and Mundesley – and very occasionally inland – which is much more difficult to find. The rather sumptuous, dusky-blue and amber spikes of the purple or yarrow broomrape are usually labelled as 'dull purple' in flower identification books. It is parasitic, attaching underground tubers to the roots of yarrow, and possibly other members of the daisy family. Its botanical name is *Orobanche purpurea*, the generic *Orobanche* being in part derived from the Greek *anche*, 'I strangle', which refers graphically to its parasitic habit. It is found in Dorset and the Isle of Wight, the Channel Isles, and Lincolnshire and is rare and threatened in all these places. Where I have seen it in Norfolk it has to face human trampling and canine fouling on clifftop paths (and mowing in a nearby churchyard) because of its proximity to fairly dense settlement. Yarrow broomrape is not found in north-east Essex and had not been seen in Suffolk for over a century when, remarkably, it was reported to have been rediscovered in the west of the county in 1992.

Sea holly.

ABOVE: Ling on the acid dunes at Winterton, Norfolk. LEFT: Sea campion. RIGHT: Yellow vetch.

LEFT: Yellow horned-poppy, Cley, Norfolk. RIGHT: Rock sea-lavender. BELOW: Sea kale at Landguard, Suffolk.

Common sea-lavender and sea purslane.

LEFT: Sea-heath and matted sea-lavender. RIGHT: Marsh mallow.

Thrift and shrubby seablite at Blakeney, Norfolk.

LEFT: Maiden pink. RIGHT: Breckland thyme.

Breckland Blooms

> Full many a Flower is born to blush unseen,
> And waste its Sweetness on the desert Air.
>
> Thomas Gray

The area we now call Breckland was once described by travellers, with sardonic but not absurd exaggeration, as the 'Great East Anglian Desert'. In the 17th century, 'travelling sands' sometimes 'quite overwhelmed some gentlemen's whole estates' and in the 18th, the country between Brandon and Mildenhall resembled a 'beaten sea coast'. Other visitors made comparisons with 'the deserts of Africa' or expanded the sea-metaphor to 'an ocean of sand'. Well into the 19th century there were estimated to be some 700 acres of inland, mobile dunes, but the most spectacular sand-blow on record took place in 1668 when untold tons from east of Lakenheath were redeposited over an area of some 1,000 acres at Santon Downham, all but burying the village and blocking the Little Ouse. Even as late as the 1880s, it is estimated that over 50,000 acres of sandy heathland remained, though we are left with not much more than 6,000 acres now. If you wish to see a surviving remnant of a mobile dune system today, you are best advised to visit the Suffolk Wildlife Trust reserve at Wangford Warren, near Brandon. Even here some artificial surface disturbance is required periodically to preserve the open sand. The lichen heath is fragile, and the reserve is not open to visitors during the spring and summer months. Scraps and scrapes of open sand persist elsewhere, for which rabbits are mainly responsible, at places such as Foxhole Heath, near Mildenhall. This site is private, but can be seen from the road.

The Breck inspires affection of an intensity greater, it seems, than apparently more picturesque areas, such as the Broads and the coast, can normally generate in their devotees. Despite the loss of the wide and distant horizons of the great expanses of heathland of the past, Breckland clings to its character and sense of difference however much it is ploughed and afforested. There is no universal agreement as to its boundaries – especially its northern limits – but even indifferent travellers rushing along the A11 road from Suffolk into Norfolk are aware that they are in it. Roughly, it covers the area of light soil derived from the sandy and gravelly deposits left following the retreat of the ice sheet: that is, not far short of 250,000 acres stretching from Swaffham almost to Bury St Edmunds and, west to east, from Lakenheath to East Harling.

The unique wildflower population of Breckland both derives from the distinctiveness of the region and contributes to it. Ecologists have identified at least five types of old grassland covering a range of soils from exposed chalk, through highly alkaline conditions colonised by calcicoles (chalk-loving species), to very acid ground at the other extreme covered with calcifuges (chalk-avoiders) such as heather or even mats of *Cladonia* lichens and mosses. But quite small acidic patches can occur alongside and amongst base-rich areas so that lime-haters and lovers grow cheek-by-jowl.

Breckland's semi-continental climate is a significant part of the explanation of why plants thrive here that are rare in, or totally absent from, the rest of the country. The climate certainly adds to the steppe-like appearance of traditional areas of the Breck, as anyone who has paid summer visits in the more drought-plagued years of the last decade can testify. The parched, browned or yellowed appearance of much of the area during the moisture-deficit months has provided a marked contrast to the capacity of much of rural Britain, including the moisture-retentive boulder clay parts of East Anglia, to keep its greenness stubbornly in dry conditions. But not only are Breckland summer daytime temperatures a little higher and annual rainfall lower than the rest of Norfolk and Suffolk (with an average of about 22 inches); the range of temperature is greater, with night frosts possible in any month of the year and recorded for an average of over 150 nights per annum. The country knows no colder lowland area than the Breck. Small wonder then that some 'steppe' plants adapted to the more extreme conditions of continental Europe are at home nowhere in Britain but here.

But human intervention in Breckland has also helped provide the habitats for some of the region's special plants. Deciduous woodland and even hedges with a mix of species are thin on the ground, and the open forest, mainly of oak, that once covered the area was cleared, it is thought, in the distant past when Neolithic man found the light soils easy to work some 4,000 years ago. The forest was replaced by heathland and the plants of disturbed ground, and sheep were grazed from Neolithic times, through the Roman period, and continuing to the end of the 19th century. Possibly this was Britain's main sheep-raising area before it declined in importance during an extended period of low wool prices in the 17th century. The Breck was described as typical 'sheep-and-rye' country, and, though much barley was also grown in the Middle Ages, areas of grassland for grazing were always retained. The practice of opening up 'breaks' or 'brecks' of stony, sandy soil in times of agricultural need or prosperity, then allowing them to revert to heathland when the nutrients were exhausted or prices fell, was ultimately to provide our name for the region.

The main challenge to the open sheepwalks came from the many enclosed rabbit warrens established on them in the Middle Ages: warrens probably covered up to 15,000 Breckland acres in the 15th century. But from a botanical point of view, the conies raised in great numbers in the warrens and the inevitable escapees who set up home in the wild, were alternative grazers to maintain and manure a close-cropped sward. They carried out this task with an efficiency all too great for some agriculturists, until myxomatosis decimated their numbers in 1954 and 1955. Since then, some grassy heaths cropped for centuries have not been thoroughly grazed, and trees have become established: the pines on Lakenheath Warren are a good example. This can present a tricky problem, for the public love trees and, quite rightly, have been so well exhorted to indignation at the destruction of rain forests abroad and village-green trees and ancient woodlands at home, that many now prefer trees invariably to the troubling wildness and seemingly empty sweep of heathland. The recent opposition to the removal of scrub from parts of Mousehold Heath, north of Norwich, is an indication of the need to reawaken the often dormant public delight in ancient open heathland.

Most areas of Breckland were cultivated during the Napoleonic wars – with a prosperous corn-growing period succeeding – and it was at this time that the planting began of the now-characteristic Breckland shelter belts and rows of Scots pine enclosing fields. Attempts were often made to keep field-boundary trees low and thick to provide better shelter without obstructing low-flying game birds, and this had the effect of allowing the build-up of a low bank of blown sand, providing a bank-and-arable-headland habitat for Breckland annuals, including three rare speedwells.

Veronica praecox barely loses out to the fingered speedwell in the dash to be the first to bloom from mid-March onwards. I suppose that logically we should call the *praecox* 'early speedwell', but East Anglia has firmly claimed it as its own under the name Breckland (or Breck) speedwell. It is possibly native, but probably not, as it was not recorded until 1933, though Simpson thought it had most likely been overlooked previously. It is found also in central and southern Europe, but nowhere in Britain outside Breckland except as a very occasional, brief casual. It grows in sandy arable fields and only half-a-dozen known sites remain in the Breck. Seed from Maidcross Hill, Lakenheath, was sown on three specially rotavated plots at the SWT Tuddenham Gallops Reserve in the Suffolk Breck. In addition, some plots were sown with fingered and spring speedwell seed at Tuddenham, and some speedwell seed together with the seed of other interesting arable weeds has also been sown since at the NWT Weeting Neath National Nature Reserve in Norfolk on land ploughed so as to simulate 'primitive' arable farming methods.

The fingered speedwell must now be the scarcest of the 'rare three' annual Breck speedwells and it was thought to survive genuinely unintroduced only on a single roadside verge site on the outskirts of Thetford until it was rediscovered near Lakenheath in 1993. It has also been sown on a couple of reserves. It is a pity it is so rare, since it is certainly native and once grew on scattered sites from Surrey to Yorkshire, including north-east Essex (only one record ever), east Suffolk, and at least 18 west Suffolk and west Norfolk Breckland parishes. To thrive on arable, the plant seems to need undisturbed, fairly open conditions during spring and cannot compete with high-density crops encouraged by sprays and fertilisers. It has been known to spring up in numbers on gravel mounds, embankments and even the gravel driveway of a Thetford bungalow. It flowers from mid-March. Extinction in the wild in Norfolk loomed in the summer of 1993 when the national housebuilder who owns the site turfed over part of it, but it was restored after timely intervention by English Nature and the Norfolk Wildlife Trust.

The third of the trio, the spring speedwell, is more common than the fingered, though that is not saying a great deal. The spring speedwell is a native of open places on dry, sandy soils, often growing with the much more common wall speedwell, for which it may be mistaken. It now occurs only in the Suffolk Breckland, but was formerly to be found also in East Suffolk and East and West Norfolk, though it has not been seen north of the Little Ouse for at least 20 years. It has a marked liking for places where rabbits have been burrowing and scratching: it therefore faced a double threat – from spraying and intensive arable farming, and the diminution in the numbers of rabbits from myxomatosis. This is the last of the trio into flower, generally not blooming before mid-April.

Our survey of Breckland speedwells culminates magnificently with the queen of them all, and a plant that has claims to the title of most beautiful Breckland species. Fittingly, it is distinct from the other rare speedwells in that it is a perennial and flowers from July to September, when the others are long gone. This is the spiked speedwell, *Veronica spicata*. In fact, it is *Veronica spicata* ssp. *spicata*, and its distinctiveness as a subspecies is for once apparent not only to botanists with hand-lenses, but also to the less meticulous wildflower aficionado. There is another subspecies, ssp. *hybrida*, which is found on limestone cliffs on the western seaboard, and has flower stems up to 60cm – twice the average stem-length of our East Anglian plant – and usually a correspondingly larger flowerhead. But its colour, compared to ssp. *spicata*, is often a disappointingly pale, even wishy-washy blue. I love to see ssp. *hybrida* growing on the great limestome whale of Humphrey Head, rising from the Furness sea-marshes and jutting out into Morecambe Bay in my native north-west, but I have to bow to the superiority of brilliant-blue ssp. *spicata* on chalky heathland in adopted East Anglia. I recall my first attempt to photograph the plant at the Norfolk Wildlife Trust's Weeting Heath NNR five years or more ago, having secured a permit from English Nature. My visit was perfectly mis-timed to coincide with a prolonged thunderstorm, the only rain for weeks before and afterwards. The warden left me to it in drenched discomfort, but the rain refused to abate. Blue flowers are normally chastened and subdued by dark clouds and dim light, retreating into the background of grasses, but the spikes of the speedwell seemed to glow defiantly, as if competing with the assertive yellow of the accompanying lady's bedstraw.

Veronica spicata ssp. *spicata*, is rarer than its western sister, being limited now to three sites in the Norfolk and Suffolk Breck and one in Cambridgeshire. It usually grows on chalk grassland, though it will tolerate slightly acid sandy conditions. Rabbits both support and threaten it in that they maintain a suitably open sward, but love to nibble the speedwell stems. At Weeting, wire-netting 'pens' were erected to exclude rabbits in the summer, but were opened up at other times of year to allow grazing. The plant can, however, flower in the face – or teeth – of limited nibbling by rabbits and mice: it spreads by stolons and can put up compensating flowers if the initial main spike is bitten off early in the season. W. G. Clarke, who coined the name 'Breckland' (or, at least, adopted it in his writings and thus assured its general acceptance), saw 1,400 massed flowering plants in 1915. But perhaps we need not despair of ever seeing such a sight in England again: after some disappointing years when such spikes as there were tended to shrivel before maturity in the drought, more than 600 blooms graced Weeting in the summer of 1993 and two new colonies were discovered in 1994.

So much for the speedwells. Currently, however, as I write in the early spring of 1996, the Tuddenham Gallops site cannot be visited for the annual species as entry onto the surrounding land is proscribed under the provisions of the Plant Health Order, 1993, because of rhizomania infection. This is a pity, as there are other Brecklanders growing on land immediately adjacent to the speedwell plots. There is Oregon grape, for example, but, more interestingly, fair quantities of cypress spurge, surely the yellowest and brightest of spurges growing outside gardens in Britain. This species is just possibly native in eastern Kent and elsewhere in south-east England, and is certainly naturalised here and there in rough grassland and waste places throughout Britain and the Channel Isles. It has been claimed that it often appears where horses are kept and trained or exercised, with the implication that seed has been imported with the foodstuffs given to the animals. Simpson's *Flora of Suffolk* yields the charming information that cypress spurge is known locally in Suffolk as welcome-to-our-house, but unfortunately does not say why. There are also some grape hyacinths growing here and there alongside the plants of cypress spurge: two rarities in rare conjunction. At one time, a third – spring speedwell – could have been found, before the spurge crowded it out.

There are, however, accessible Breckland specialities to be seen in the neighbourhood alongside the public roads. A walk from Tuddenham village west along the minor road leading to the Cherry Hill/Herringswell Road crossroads first yields a Suffolk Wildlife Trust protected roadside verge marked with posts. Wild grape hyacinth, *Muscari neglectum* (which in its time has also been called *M. atlanticum* and *M. racemosum*), also blooms here in April and May, though not all plants of this perennial species flower every year. As you will readily see from this site, it is a plant of dry chalky and sandy grassland, often growing on open roadside verges and banks, or hedgerow banks. It is native to Suffolk and Cambridgeshire, but very local there, and is long extinct in Norfolk, though it did once grow in the Harleston area. It is naturalised in other parts of southern Britain, but is rare and, in any case, the garden grape hyacinth, *Muscari armeniacum* is often mistaken for it. The garden species, so widely escaped in Breckland, is a fairly uniform brighter blue. The true wild plant has fertile flowers of a colour ranging from a dark violet to an almost blackish blue, with white lobes: the 'grape' appellation fits it, as regards colour, much more convincingly. The sterile flowers are smaller and of a paler blue. The wild grape or starch hyacinth itself (its flowers smell of wet starch) also sometimes escapes from gardens into the wild, though it is actually rarely grown today.

Continue walking along the road and past the plantation on your left until you reach the crossroads, where there are more roadside verge reserves, and arable headlands purposely left wide and unused by the farmer. You may well be able to see Breckland speedwell and other interesting arable weeds from the road.

One rare arable weed not to be found near Tuddenham Gallops is small alison. It is sometimes incorrectly called hoary alison, the English name for the alien *Berteroa incana* from south-east Europe, which occasionally appears as a casual. In the early 1980s, small alison survived on one Breck site only alongside, and sometimes upon, a farm track running next to a shelter belt of pine and beech through arable fields. It is a low-growing annual of the cabbage family with tiny pale-yellow flowers from April to June. It is generally accepted to be an introduced species from Europe and western Asia, though Simpson wondered if it might be native to the Breck and Sandlings. It was formerly widespread in southern and eastern Britain, including Norfolk, as a casual, but it persisted from year to year in Suffolk. It was declared a scheduled and protected species under the provisions of the Wildlife and Countryside Act of 1981 and the second edition of the *Red Data Book (Vascular Plants)* in 1983 placed it at the top of its 'Threat Number' scale of 1-13 (13 indicating species closest to extinction). The problem is one of extreme sensitivity to modern farming methods and particularly to spray drift. The plant is said to hang on by its fingernails in the Sandlings, though I have never seen it there. I made the diversion from the A11 to the Suffolk Breck site more than once in years gone by, but of late the Suffolk Wildlife Trust has very justifiably appealed to those in the know to refrain from visiting the few remaining small alison and perennial knawel sites, and from disclosing their whereabouts to others.

My account so far might lead a stranger to Breckland to imagine it now consists of arable farmland and shelter belts, with remnants of old sheepwalks and rabbit warrens surviving as isolated bits of heathland. But in fact huge tracts have been transformed to other uses and purposes. Thetford Forest, a Forestry Commission holding, covers some 51,500 acres or 80 square miles, and is mainly Scots and Corsican pinewood, with some very limited amenity deciduous planting. It is the largest forest in England, and swallowed up the heart of the old heathy Breckland. Some of the old Breck plants thrive along trackways and rides, and the unspectacular rupturewort has seemingly increased markedly, but one struggles to think of many plants of distinction fostered by the forest itself. Yet, ironically, it is the forest that probably attracts the visitor to Breckland more than any other single feature today.

The other great devourers of the Breck have been the military, though golf courses and urban development have also gobbled their share. The American (though nominally RAF) air base at Lakenheath took a deal of Lakenheath Warren, but a far larger appropriation was the 12,600-acre chunk of Breckland that became the Stanford Training Area. This turned out to be a wildlife blessing on balance, since it meant the land outside the actual camps was preserved from other depradations and public access, and became largely sheep-grazed grassland when not suffering disturbance from army exercises. Unfortunately, the grassland is almost all reverted arable, which does not – yet? – contain the interesting and rare Breckland flowers, and even scraps of genuinely old chalky grassland are bare of these real rarities. Visually, though, parts of this open, stony, sparsely-vegetated area are poignant reminders of the heaths and reverted brecks of old.

The perimeter fence of the American air base now stands within yards of a good assemblage of rare plants, some of which are found only in Breckland. Maidcross Hill, above Lakenheath, is a curious survival, for farmers brought ploughs here to perform the time-honoured practice of polishing the shares by pulling them through the gravelly earth, as sophisticated military aeroplanes took off and landed yards away. Many pits remain where the gravel was extracted. The site is owned by Elveden Farms Ltd and access is by permission only, from the Estate Office.

Round some of the pits, plants of Spanish catchfly grow in fair numbers, though not massed like a 'hay crop', as W. G. Clarke once saw them in Breckland. This is a good example of a continental steppe plant, preferring shallow, dry soils, growing at its north-west limited, for it occurs nowhere else in Britain except as an occasional casual. In Breckland, it is a native of dry, grassy heathland, and is capable of reproducing vegetatively when competing with quite thick, tall grasses, but can reproduce from seed only in more open chalky-sandy conditions, where seed can fall on some bare earth, caused by rabbits or perhaps by human intervention, as at Maidcross. Even vehicles driving onto roadside verges can produce the right conditions, as sometimes happens to the often-littered verges of the north side of the B1112 road at Foxhole Heath. It is an unassertive plant, more likely to interest you in the stickiness of its slender stem rising from a basal rosette of leaves than its small, yellowish-cream flowers in apparent whorls, with stamens and styles often on different plants. Spanish catchfly also grows wild in Norfolk, though on only three remaining sites.

A relation of the catchfly dwells close by at Maidscross Hill, but is a little more quaint, with, usually, bright-pink small flowers atop a sepal-tube that soon swells so as to seem out of all proportion to the petals. The prominent veining of this tube gives the plant its alternative common name of striated catchfly, though it is more usually called sand catchfly because of its preference for inland or coastal disturbed sandy conditions. This annual, producing viable seed in quantity in hot summers, cannot claim to be peculiar to the Breck, but it is only very locally found in parts of eastern and southern Britain and the Channel Isles, and seems to be decreasing in East Anglia except in Breckland. It has been found in our region outside the Breck as far north as Sheringham on the Norfolk Coast (where it still grows at Beeston Regis) and as far south-east as Landguard Common (SWT) at the tip of Suffolk. It now has only four inland and three coastal sites in Norfolk, but has appeared with the bur medick on chalky verges of the newish Thetford bypass. At the Haven, Thorpeness (another SWT reserve), it is to be found duplicating the Maidscross Hill association with bur medick, suffocated clover and clustered clover. As well as its sandy coastal sites, sand catchfly grows inland in East Anglia alongside tracks across heaths, on sandy field margins and in arable fields.

Among other unusual plants at Maidscross Hill is small cudweed, and the wild grape hyacinth has been found on boundary banks adjacent to arable fields. Common star-of-Bethleham also appears in similar conditions in the locality, but profusely-flowering garden throwouts are notoriously easy to confuse with the wild plant, which is thought to be native in Britain probably only in eastern England. The wild *Ornithogalum umbellatum* is much more shy, sometimes refusing to flower at all. *Ornithogalum* implies the plant is comparable to a white bird.

An interesting Maidscross plant is the small medick, which grows in ground-hugging mats, with plants of sand catchfly growing through it here and there, miniaturised by the windy, open situation of some parts of the Hill. I prefer the name bur medick for this long-flowering little yellow medick which carries interesting bur seedheads at the same time as the later flowers.

There are in fact more medicks and other members of the *Leguminosae* or pea family of interest in Breckland. The violet flowers of Lucerne, *Medicago sativa*, ssp. *sativa*, sometimes sown as a fodder crop, are fairly familiar. This species is also known as alfalfa or purple medick, and originated in the Mediterranean region. It sometimes appears as a relic of cultivation on field margins, rough grassland, and waste places. But the yellow-flowered perennial sickle medick, *Medicago sativa* ssp. *falcata* is a native plant – though only in East Anglia. Rationally enough, it is also known as yellow medick. It is to be found fairly frequently in Breckland (and less commonly near the coast) on dry roadsides and chalk grassland, though it does not survive grazing by rabbits. It once appeared in north-east Essex on a sea wall at Manningtree, but almost certainly the seeds had come from a nearby seed merchant. The two subspecies sometimes cross to produce a plant of extraordinary colour variation, now thought by many botanists to merit subspecies status as *Medicago sativa* ssp. *varia* because of its independent existence in many localities and use as a crop in continental Europe. It is partly fertile and there seem to be back-crosses with the parent subspecies from time to time.

If the descriptions seem to obscure the plants, why not stop and see them in their clear-cut and attractive reality at one of the roadside sites? The so-called Icklingham Triangle, well-known to Breckland botanists, is a good one. This is a small area of rough grassland tucked between a track forming the base of the triangle and the A1101 and B1112 roads coverging to form the apex. My research suggests reassuringly that, though wildflower aficionados undoubtedly desert hearth and home to botanize in the Icklingham Triangle, none has so far disappeared mysteriously there. The B1112 side of the triangle continues as an SWT roadside verge reserve, and in a good year you can see plants of bright yellow sickle medick, but also, sprawling and mingling in a promiscuous hotbed of hybrid vigour, sand Lucerne or hybrid wild medick (that is ssp. *varia*) in a lovely variety of colours that may range from pale yellow-green to pale mauve, blue, purple and near-black.

A less scarce but still notable member of the pea family is the purple milk-vetch, which is confined to the Breck in our region. It is perhaps the most handsome of the Breckland peaflowers, producing its bluish-purple flowers locally on dry, sandy banks, waysides and heaths where chalk is present. It is quite cosmopolitan, growing as far away as Sutherland in Scotland and the Aran Isles in County Clare, though it is more plentiful in the drier east of Britain than the west. A particularly extensive, ground-hugging patch on Foxhole Heath close to the wire fence is often so striking in late May that passing motorists could be forgiven for assuming a mass escape of garden *Aubrieta*.

There remain one or two rarities surviving as natives only in Breckland. Field wormwood is a local perennial of the Breck which used also to appear from time to time in other parts of Norfolk, Suffolk and Cambridgeshire: in fact, a plant was found not far from East Dereham by the roadside in 1992. There is an introduced colony naturalised on the Crymlyn Burrows sand dunes in Glamorgan, but, jealous of our own, we of course do not count that! When one sees a plant in flower in August or September, it appears quite sturdy and vigorous, but in fact young plants are sensitive to rabbit grazing and cannot compete with tall grasses: low-competition fallow land or open spaces with some bare ground are required, and the plant is restricted to sandy heaths in the Breck. It has also suffered grievously from human intervention in the way of building development and traffic driving over verges on which it was established. In fact, the best site to see it now is a curious little SWT reserve tucked away, like a vacant plot ripe for development, amongst the factory, warehouse and office units of an industrial estate alongside the A1065 on the southern outskirts of Brandon. It also grows on Thetford Heath, but there is no public access. It seems now to have only one Norfolk station near Thetford.

More pleasantly, the plant is sometimes called field southernwood, but it lacks the aromatic nature of most of the other British wormwoods, including even the common-or-graden mugwort. Rather interestingly, the bitter wormwood itself, found a little more widely than field southernwood as a naturalised species in East Anglia, was used to treat parasitic worms mainly as a consequence of its name. 'Wormwood' in fact derives from an Old English name, *wermod*, of obscure significance, but unrelated to worms. For it to work as a vermifuge, you need such a large dose of wormwood that it becomes alarmingly dangerous. The volatile oil it contains can, in quantity, work as a violent poison producing vertigo, cramps, intoxication and delerium. Prolonged use can lead to madness!

Everyone knows the aromatic, rosy mats of thyme, yet frequent changes in classification and nomenclature have made a botanical jungle of a familiar little plant to bemuse those wildflower novices who plunge into attempts to identify the different species. It is a good game and an uncertain flutter to try to open two floras in succession which tell the same tale. But at least it can be asserted that there is a species of thyme – Breckland thyme – which is a native of sandy heaths and has been found on 20 sites or more in the Breck, though it once also grew in Cambridgeshire. In Norfolk, it is now down to three sites only, including a plentiful show near Thetford Warren Lodge. The latest of the authoritative floras tells us its scientific name is *Thymus serpyllum* and that it closely resembles wild thyme, *Thymus polytrichus* (which in its time has also been called *Thymus drucei*, *Thymus praecox* – and *Thymus serpyllum*!), but is usually a little smaller. The best way to tell the difference is to look at a flowering stem and scrutinize the hairs thereon: Breckland thyme has fairly rounded stems with hairs more or less equally all round, but wild thyme has square stems with hairs more or less limited to two opposite faces. But beware – Breckland thyme is rare, and wild thyme is also a local chalk grassland species in the Breck. The species you are most likely to come across in the area is the more robust large or greater thyme, *Thymus pulegioides*, which is the strongest-scented of the three. This has hairs more or less only on the four angles of the stem. It can compete with quite thick, ungrazed heath grass, whereas Breckland thyme likes bare patches in short, open turf.

'Thyme' comes, ultimately and obscurely, from the ancient Greek and has nothing to do directly with the passage of time, though, rather distressingly, this easily-loved little plant does evoke thoughts of the Grim Reaper in that it was planted on graves in Wales and was sometimes placed in a house after a death or carried at the funeral. The souls of the dead – especially those murdered – dwell in its flowers and its scent lingers sometimes at the site of the foul deed. There are positive attributes: it is also paradoxically a symbol of strength and

ABOVE: Wild grape hyacinth and cypress spurge growing among spring beauty near Tuddenham, Suffolk. LEFT: Spiked speedwell among lady's bedstraw on Weeting Heath, Norfolk. RIGHT: A 'continental' Brecklander: Spanish catchfly at Lakenheath, Suffolk. BELOW: The military orchid flowering in early June near Barton Mills, Suffolk.

can induce a vision of a woman's husband-to-be. It is pleasant to think its name may derive from the Greek word for incense, though, equally pleasingly, it could come from *thymos*, 'courage', because of its stimulating, encouraging aroma. One is aware of it often before one sees it, and no scent is more evocative: the poet T. S. Eliot endows 'the wild thyme unseen' with the power of transporting us to a 'moment in and out of time'. Its culinary virtue, as one of the most familiar European herbs, is versatile and undisputed and it has medicinal applications in that infusions have been used to relieve whooping cought and bronchitis and, externally, to heal wounds. It can be included in herbal baths and cushions.

One of the least spectacular Breckland rarities is, in one respect, the most remarkable. This is perennial knawel, which is not very different from annual knawel, a more widespread plant in Breckland. The perennial knawel is *Scleranthus perennis* ssp. *prostratus*, which is found nowhere else in the world than the Breck, though there is another subspecies, ssp. *perennis*, growing on rocks in Radnorshire, which is not endemic. By the mid-1980s, the Breckland plant was reduced to four Suffolk colonies and a Site of Special Scientific Interest where it was possible to take conservation measures: now it seems only one site remains. It did once grow in Norfolk, including a couple of distant non-Breckland sites at the Walsey Hills, Cley and at Snettisham gravel pits, where it was probably introduced. It was indisputably introduced to Thetford Heath, to which there is no public admission. It will grow on rather bare ground (including the compacted soil of tracks), dry sand heaths with some short vegetation, and fallow or abandoned arable fields – and it likes a slightly more acid soil than most of the other Breckland rarities. Agricultural and housing development have posed the principal threat to the survival of the knawel.

Perennial knawel is a member of the pink family, but much more attractive to the general wildflower-lover is the perennial maiden pink, many forms of which have found their way into our gardens, principally as rock-garden plants. The maiden pink is by no means exclusive to East Anglia, let alone Breckland, but it is an attractive species that is found on scattered dry grassland, heath and rocky outcrop sites in Britain, north to central and north-east Scotland, and is decreasing. In our region it is now chiefly confined to chalky Breckland heaths. Pinks are highly-connected: the generic name *Dianthus* means 'flower of Zeus (or Jove)' and the specific *deltoides* refers to the fact that the pale pink white-centred, spotted petals with an irregular circle of reddish-pink, are shaped like the Greek letter delta. Surprisingly, the colour pink derives its name from the flowers of the genus; not the other way round. The flowers themselves in fact got their name from a fancied resemblance to the 'pinks' or ornamental openings in Elizabethan dress. A well-known Breckland site for maiden pink is the Weeting Heath National Nature Reserve, but if you wish to see it without any access complications, a few plants persist at Ramparts Field between Icklingham and West Stow, where you can park and picnic. There is also a nice display of meadow saxifrage there.

Another species of pink, once thought to be a casual in the Norfolk Breck, has been claimed very recently as an overlooked native of inland west Norfolk by Gillian Beckett and John Akeroyd. This is the inconspicuous, rather tongue-twistingly alliterative proliferous pink, with its dense clusters of small flowers, only one or two of which are open at a time. The proliferous pink, despite some confusion with a closely-related species, was recorded here and there in the Norfolk Breck up to 1950, but was then not seen again until 1985, in a colony at Cranwich, where 70 plants were growing in 1992.

Maiden pinks often grow on barish patches, and another species sometimes founded on bare or disturbed ground is the scarce wall bedstraw. It has been recorded on arable and disturbed land, such as Barnhamcross Common, though this a rarer habitat than bare chalkpit sides and chalk rubble. But this small, weak annual, flowering in June and July, is easier to find, as its name hints, on old flint mortar walls and sometimes on gravel at the foot of such walls. It has, in its time, been found on well-known ancient structures in Breckland such as Weeting Castle and the Nunnery, Thetford, as well as more anonymous old walls in many Breckland towns and villages. Try Little Cressingham churchyard west of Watton in Norfolk. New sites at Heacham and Feltwell were discovered in 1993.

Wall bedstraw is found as a native now only in south-east and south central England and Breckland is its British heartland, though it is most common in the Mediterranean region. It has been recorded in some 16 tetrads in the Norfolk and Suffolk Breck since 1970. *Scarce Plants in Britain* wonders whether the fact it is reportedly found on west Norfolk walls almost all of ancient origin might support suggestions that it spread northwards in Europe during a warmer era between 1150 and 1300, and has been decreasing outside its south European stronghold ever since.

The plant that can claim to be the greatest Breckland rarity in terms of fewest sites ever found in East Anglia is the ground-pine, which was recorded by Alec Bull in 1948 on the edge of a dry field at West Stow, and was still there in 1979. There are no other records in our region, and it has not been seen at West Stow since the field changed its owner and use some time ago. This annual of bare stony ground – often arable field margins – or sparsely grassy habitats, preferring calcareous soils, often takes advantage of rabbits creating scrapes and nibbling back the competing crops. It tends to make only sporadic flowerings even at its regular sites, which may be in large part due to seedlings from autumn germinations succumbing to long, wet, cold winters. Certainly, plants seen at its West Stow site varied through the years from thousands down to a couple and even none at all.

Ground-pine is a curious little plant with yellow flowers marked red or purple and leaves each of three narrow lobes, which are indeed slightly reminiscent of conifer leaves. Furthermore, it exudes a faint smell of pine resin, despite being a herb of the labiate or mint family. It seems unlikely that ground-pine, a lover of warm soils growing here at the extreme edge of its range and vulnerable to modern arable farming regimes, will now be found on other Breckland sites. Plantlife are trying to preserve it nationally at its most threatened stations.

Another rarity grows on the Breckland fringe and is neither a dry heathland plant nor an arable weed. Berry catchfly is an extremely rare perennial alien campion which has in the past appeared as a casual elsewhere, but which persists in rough grass, hedgerows and plantations now only in a limited area of west Norfolk – in particular around Merton village and at the private Hills and Holes site near Great Hockham. It is a central- and southern-European plant which often scrambles through shrubs and other vegetation. The flowers, which do not come until late July, are greenish white, but a large, gleaming black berry eventually forms in each one. The species was first noticed in the area in 1914, but had been known on the Isle of Dogs for a hundred years, though it has long since disappeared from this site. I remember searching for the plant along the public road near the gates of Lord Walsingham's park at Merton, when he drove by and, being used to botanists rummaging in his hedgerows, stopped and directed me to one of its stations. The story is that a forbear noticed that pheasants in Hungary liked the berries and returned home with some plants, which he established in estate woodland. The seeds are dispersed by bird carriage, and it appears that Norfolk pheasants are continuing the good work of distributing the plant a little more widely to this day.

There remain other Breckland specialities, such as *Viola tricolor* ssp. *Curtisii*, the form of wild pansy which normally grows on maritime dunes, but, curiously, occurs also by inland lakes in Northern Ireland and on the sandy heaths of Breckland and the Sandlings. The less scarce form of wild pansy, though itself not common these days, is more widely distributed in East Anglia. It is associated with kissing – a Norfolk name is kiss-me-over-the-garden-gate and it was known as kiss-at-the-garden-gate (or Jack-behind-the-garden-gate) in Suffolk – and the more usual name, heartsease, indicates the relief that kissing brings to the ardent lover.

A fairly common plant characteristic of sandy and chalky ground and arable field margins in Breckland is the beautiful viper's bugloss, with its flowers in branched spikes turning from pink in the bud to vivid blue, though they are occasionally white. It was once known locally as bluebottle in Norfolk, a name more often applied to the cornflower, but was more generally cat's tail in East Anglia. The species is not to be taken as attractive to or utilised by adders, but rather as curing and even preventing snakebite. It is allegedly efficacious in increasing the flow of mothers' milk and easing lumbago, and a syrup derived from the plant has been thought useful in combatting melancholia.

Tower mustard, which is scarce elsewhere, has increased significantly in limited areas on light, sandy soil of the Norfolk Breck in recent years, especially in clear-felled coniferous plantations, and two scarce arable-weed fumitories, *Fumaria densiflora* and *Fumaria parviflora* are also found in the Breck. The generic name is from the Latin for 'smoke of the earth', referring either to the diffuse foliage or the old assertion that the juice of the plant, like smoke, makes you weep if it gets in your eyes – or possibly to both explanations. The first species, dense-flowered fumitory, is found also on East Anglian calcareous clays to the south-west of the Breck, but fine-leaved fumitory is more wholeheartedly a Breck plant, growing in an arc of tetrads from the eastern side of the Wash down through west Norfolk, on through Breckland, and curving south-west out of our region.

It so happens that the queen – or perhaps strictly it should be the king – of East Anglian orchids also grows in Breckland. The military or soldier orchid was not even recorded as a member of our regional flora before 1954 when a colony of about 500 plants – much the largest in Britain – was discovered in a long-disused Suffolk chalkpit in the Butt Plantation of the Forestry Commission Mildenhall Woods. The species had been fairly frequent before the late 19th century in an arc of English counties south and west of our region, but was then thought to be extinct until rediscovered in the Buckinghamshire Chilterns in 1947. The Suffolk orchids grow at a considerable distance from the other two extant British sites in a dampish pit, eight metres high and about 25 across, now known as the Rex Graham Reserve. It is security-fenced to foil depredations by criminal orchid collectors, but the Suffolk Wildlife Trust stages an open day annually, usually on a Saturday in early June, when admirers may view the orchids from a wooden catwalk.

To check a diminution of plants from a 1958 'high' of over 2,500 to approximately 250 by 1971, the clearing or cutting-back of various bushes and the more invasive common herbs was undertaken, and pines to the south were felled to re-admit lost sunlight. By the start of the 1990s, 1,100 plants were present with almost 300 flowering spikes, and a chalky depression has been scraped out near the pit in the hope of providing a habitat for seedling orchids. The pit is also a site for twayblade and the wonderfully-scented mezerion, which would be the species to ensure the pit's fame were it not for the co-presence and surpassing glamour of the military orchid.

Orchis militaris is called the military or soldier orchid because its vanilla-scented flowers were thought to resemble a human figure, with the upper sepals and petals forming a large pointed hood allegedly like an old-fashioned soldier's helmet. This is pale lilac on the outside, with a whitish cast, and the inner surfaces have parallel stripes of purple or dark green. The pinkish four-lobed lip forms the body and limbs of the soldier, with small, dark-red spots representing the buttons of the tunic, though it cannot be claimed that they display the perfect symmetry of military orderliness. The stem usually stands quite erect and sturdy, as befits the plant's soldierly status.

As a footnote to the finding of the military orchid and to underline Suffolk's reputation for providing orchid surprises, it should be mentioned that a single plant of the early spider orchid was discovered in the Suffolk Breck in 1991. This species had occurred with any regularity only on chalk grassland and calcareous pastures south of the Thames for many years and had not been seen in Suffolk for 200 years, nor in north-east Essex since 1700, where it once grew with man orchids in Belchamp St Paul and in an old Ballingdon gravel pit. Norfolk's closest attempt to rival Suffolk in the Breckland rare orchid stakes was provided by the finding of the green-flowered helleborine just within the county at Sanford in 1969, though some experts subsequently suspected the plants to be a form of the broad-leaved helleborine.

There is one nationally-scarce plant sufficiently widespread and assertive in the Breck to contribute significantly to its character. Sandy or gravelly tracks – and car parks – where vehicles have consolidated the surface and where there is some autumn and winter dampness, are good places to look, but you will not have to look hard in summer if the plant is present, for great patches of crimson will be produced by the tiny leaves and stems of packed plants of mossy stonecrop, sometimes known as mossy tillaea, and, as its name suggests, a moss-like annual carpeting the ground. In spring, its mats are yellow-green. It thrives in places devoid of other vegetation and will tolerate slightly acid conditions. It is quite common also on the Norfolk Greensand belt close to the Wash coast and on the east Suffolk heaths, such as Hollesley, Iken and Westleton. Simpson's *Flora of Suffolk* describes it as frequent, and the *Flora of Norfolk* asserts more sweepingly that scarcely a Breckland track is without it. It is pleasant to end with a diminutive species that seems to have increased its sites and its populations in East Anglia in response to modern practices and conditions.

LEFT: Fingered speedwell. RIGHT: Common star-of-Bethlehem.
BELOW: Breckland Speedwell.

Breckland lichens and mobile sand at Wangford Warren, Suffolk.

LEFT: Sickle medick. CENTRE: Green-flowered helleborine. RIGHT:
Field wormwood. BELOW: Berry catchfly.

ABOVE: Bur medick. BELOW: Mossy stonecrop.

SELECT BIBLIOGRAPHY

Armstrong, Patrick *The Changing Landscape. The History and Ecology of Man's Impact on the Face of East Anglia* (Terence Dalton 1975)
Baker, Margaret *Discovering the Folklore of Plants* (Shire 1969)
Beardsall, Charles & Casey, Dorothy *Suffolk's Changing Landscape. Wildlife Habitats and their Conservation* (Suffolk Wildlife Trust 1995)
Blamey, Marjorie & Grey-Wilson, Christopher *The Illustrated Flora of Britain & Northern Europe* (Hodder & Stoughton 1989)
Chadwick, Lee *In Search of Heathland* (Dobson 1982)
Clarke, W. G. *In Breckland Wilds* (EP Publishing 1974; reprint of 1937 second edition)
Coleburn, Phil & Gibbons, Bob *Britain's Countryside Heritage. A Guide to the Landscape* (Blandford 1990)
Coombs, A. J. *The Collingridge Dictionary of Plant Names* (Collingridge 1985)
Corke, David *The Nature of Essex. The Wildlife & Ecology of the County* (Barracuda Books 1984)
Edlin, Herbert L. (ed.) *East Anglian Forests. Forestry Commission Guide* (HMSO 1972)
Ellis, E. A. *The Broads* (Collins 1965)
Ellis, E. A. *The Countryside of East Anglia* (Jarrold 1979)
Evans, Ros *Nature Guide to East Anglia & Lincolnshire* (Usborne 1981)
Fitter, R. and A., & Blamey, M. *The Wildflowers of Britain & Northern Europe* (Collins 1985; fourth edition)
Fluck, Hans (trans. Rowson, J. M.) *Medicinal Plants* (W. Foulsham 1976)
George, Martin *The Land Use, Ecology & Conservation of Broadland* (Packard Publishing 1992)
Grigson, Geoffrey *A Dictionary of English Plant Names* (Allen Lane 1973)
Grigson, Geoffrey *The Englishman's Flora* (Dent 1958)
Gunton, Tony (ed.) *Essex Wildlife Trust Nature Reserves Handbook* (Essex Wildlife Trust 1992)
Hyan, Roger & Pankhurst, Richard *Plants and Their Names: A Concise Dictionary* (Oxford University Press 1995)
Hywel-Davies, J., Thorn, V. & Bennett, L. *The Macmillan Guide to Britain's Nature Reserves* (Macmillan 1986; new edition)
Jessup, George *Breckland Ramblings* (George Reeve 1992)
Lang, David *A Guide to the Wild Orchids of Great Britain & Ireland* (Oxford University Press 1989; second edition)
Launert, Edmund *Edible and Medicinal Plants of Britain & Northern Europe* (Hamlyn 1981)
Linsell, Stewart *Hickling Broad & its Wildlife* (Terence Dalton 1990)
Mabey, Richard *Food for Free* (Harper Collins 1989; 'all colour edition')
Mabey, Richard *Plants with a Purpose* (Fontana 1979)
Mabey, Richard & Evans, Tony *The Flowering of Britain* (Arrow 1982)
Manning, S. A. *Nature in East Anglia* (World's Work 1976)
Marsden, David *Nature Watcher's Directory* (Hamlyn 1984)
Moore, Derek (ed.) *Watching Wildlife in Suffolk. A New Guide to the County's Nature Reserves* (Suffolk Wildlife Trust 1994)
Nature in Norfolk: A Heritage in Trust (Jarrold 1976)
Norfolk Wildlife Trust Reserves Handbook, 1995 (Norfolk Wildlife Trust 1995)
Norwich & its Region (British Association for the Advancement of Science 1961)
Perring, F. H. & Farrell, L. *British Red Data Books 1: Vascular Plants* (Royal Society for Nature Conservation 1983; second edition)
Perring, F. H. & Walters, S. M. *Atlas of the British Flora* (Nelson 1962)
Petch, C. P. & Swann, E. L. *Flora of Norfolk* (Jarrold 1968)
Phillips, Roger *Wild Food* (Macmillan 1983)
Rackham, Oliver *The History of the Countryside* (Dent 1986)
Rackham, Oliver *Trees & Woodland in the British Landscape* (Weidenfield & Nicolson 1995; revised edition)
Rose, Francis *The Wild Flower Key* (Warne 1981)
Salisbury, E. J. *The East Anglian Flora: A Study in Comparative Plant Geography* (Norfolk & Norwich Naturalists' Society 1932)
Sanford, Martin *The Orchids of Suffolk: an Atlas and History* (Suffolk Naturalists' Society 1991)
Simpson, Francis W. *Simpson's Flora of Suffolk* (Suffolk Naturalists' Society 1982)
Stace, Clive *New Flora of the British Isles* (Cambridge University Press 1991)
Stearn, William T. *Botanical Latin* (Nelson 1994; fourth edition)
Sterry, Paul *Regional Wildlife: Norfolk Broads* (Dial House 1995)
Stevens, John E. *Discovering Wild Plant Names* (Shire 1973)
Stewart A., Pearman, D. A. & Preston, C. D. *Scarce Plants in Britain* (Joint Nature Conservation Committee 1994)
Swann, E. L. *Supplement to the Flora of Norfolk* (F. Crowe & Sons 1975)
Tarpey, Terri & Heath, Jerry *Wild Flowers of North East Essex* (Colchester Natural History Society 1990)
Trist, P. J. O. *An Ecological Flora of Breckland* (EP Publishing 1979)
Vickery, Roy *A Dictionary of Plant Lore* (Oxford University Press 1995)

PLANT INDEX

All figures in *italics* refer to illustrations.

Species	Scientific name	
Aaron's rod	*Verbascum thapsus*	29
Aconite, Winter	*Eranthis hyemalis*	50,*71*
Agrimony, Hemp	*Eupatorium cannabinum*	80
Alder	*Alnus glutinosa*	50,52,75
Alfalfa	*Medicago sativa* ssp. *sativa*	125
Alison Hoary	*Berteroa incana*	123
Small	*Alyssum alyssoides*	123
Anemone, Wood	*Anemone nemorosa*	16,23,48,50,51, 52,*65*
Angelica	*Angelica sylvestris*	80
Archangel, Red	*Lamium purpureum*	55
Yellow	*Lamiastrum galeobdolon*	48,55
Arrowhead	*Sagittaria sagittifolia*	77,85,95
Ash	*Fraxinus excelsior*	46,55,58,63,75
Asphodel, Bog	*Narthecium ossifragum*	89,98
Aster, Sea	*Aster tripolium*	90,*100*,108
Aubrieta	*Aubrieta deltoidea*	125
Avens, Water	*Geum rivale*	57,*57*
x Avens, Wood	*Geum x intermedium*	56
Wood	*Geum urbanum*	55
Bacon-and-eggs	*Lotus corniculatus*	111
Beauty, Spring	*Claytonia perfoliata*	*127*
Bedstraw, Fen	*Galium uliginosum*	80
Lady's	*Galium verum*	16,24,55,103, 122,*127*
Wall	*Galium parisiense*	129
Beech	*Fagus sylvatica*	58,59
Beet, Sea	*Beta vulgaris* ssp. *maritima*	104
Bellflower, Clustered	*Campanula glomerata*	22
Bells, Coventry	*Pulsatilla vulgaris*	23
Dead-men's	*Fritillaria meleagris*	15
Fairies'	*Convallaria majalis*	59
Pentecostal	*Hyacinthoides non-scripta*	53
-of-Sodom, Drooping	*Fritillaria meleagris*	14
Mournful	*Fritillaria meleagris*	14
Solemn	*Fritillaria meleagris*	14
Doleful	*Fritillaria meleagris*	14
Bindweed, Black	*Fallopia convolvulus*	77
Field	*Convolvulus arvensis*	103
Sea	*Calystegia soldanella*	103,*110*
Birch	*Betula pendula*	75
Bishop, Five-faced	*Adoxa moschatellina*	52
Bittersweet	*Solanum dulcamara*	77
Bladderwort, Common	*Utricularia vulgaris*	86,96
Greater	*Utricularia vulgaris*	86
Blind-eyes	*Papaver rhoeas*	31
-man	*Papaver rhoeas*	31
Blindy-buffs	*Papaver rhoeas*	31
Bloody-warrior	*Fritillaria meleagris*	14
Bluebell	*Hyacinthoides non-scripta*	44,48,52,53,55
Bluebottle	*Centaurea cyanus*	30,130
Bogbean	*Menyanthes trifoliata*	90,98
Bonnet, Granny's	*Aquilegia vulgaris*	83
Bonnets, Ladies'	*Aquilegia vulgaris*	83
Boodle	*Chrysanthemum segetum*	30
Boys, Naked	*Colchium autumnale*	17
Bracken	*Pteridium aquilinum*	87
Brandy-bottle	*Nuphar lutea*	73
Broad-arrow	*Sagittaria sagittifolia*	77,85
Brookline	*Veronica beccabunga*	77
Broom	*Cytisus scoparius*	20,87
Broomrape, Common	*Orobanche minor*	31,*42*
Purple	*Orobanche purpurea*	*110*,111
Yarrow	*Orobanche purpurea*	111,112
Buckbean	*Menyanthes trifoliata*	90
Buddle	*Chrysanthemum segetum*	30
Bugle	*Ajuga reptans*	24,48,55,59,67
Bugloss, Viper's	*Echium vulgare*	130
Bundweed	*Succisa pratensis*	82
Burnet, Salad	*Sanguisorba minor*	14
Butcher, Blue	*Orchis mascula*	18
Buttercup, Celery-leaved	*Ranunculus sceleratus*	77,91
Goldilocks	*Ranunculus auricomus*	16
Butterwort, Common	*Pinguicula vulgaris*	13,14,20,*34*,89, 98

Species	Scientific name	
Calamint, Common	*Clinopodium ascendens*	28
Lesser	*Clinopodium calamintha*	28,*40*
Campion, Red	*Silene dioica*	26,55
Sea	*Silene uniflora*	26,104,*113*
Candlemass-plant	*Verbascum thapsus*	29
Canker	*Papaver rhoeas*	31
Carrot, Wild	*Daucus carota*	105
Cat's-tail	*Echium vulgare*	130
Catchfly, Berry	*Cucubalus baccifer*	129,134
Sand	*Silene conica*	124,125
Spanish	*Silene otites*	124,*127*
Striated	*Silene conica*	124
Catsear, Common	*Hypochaeris radicata*	103
Celandine, Lesser	*Ranunculus ficaria*	48,*64*
Centuary, Common	*Centaurium erythraea*	103,105
Lesser	*Centarium pulchellum*	104
Small	*Centarium pulchellum*	104
Chaff, Red	*Papaver rhoeas*	31
Charlock	*Sinapsis arvensis*	30
Chickweed, Water	*Myosoton aquaticum*	90,99
Cinquefoil, Marsh	*Potentilla palustris*	90,99
Clock, Town-hall	*Adoxa moschatellina*	52
Clover, Bird's-foot	*Trifolium ornithopodioides*	107
Burrowing	*Trifolium subterraneum*	25
Clustered	*Trifolium glomeratum*	107,124
Hare's-foot	*Trifolium arvense*	25
Marsh	*Menyanthes trifoliata*	90
Sea	*Trifolium squamosum*	107
Strawberry	*Trifolim fragiferum*	25
Suffocated	*Trifolium suffocatum*	25,107,124
Sulphur	*Trifolium ochroleucon*	19,25,26,28
White	*Trifolium repens*	31
Cockerel	*Agrostemma githago*	30
Cods	*Orchis mascula*	18
Columbine	*Aquilegia vulgaris*	72,83
Convolvulus, Sea	*Calystegia soldanella*	103
Cord-grass	*Spartina sp.*	102
Corncockle	*Agrostemma githago*	30
Cornflower	*Centaurea cyanus*	30,31,130
Couch, Sand	*Elymus farctus*	102
Sea	*Elymus pycnanthus*	102
Cow-wheat, Common	*Melampyrum pratense*	52,61
Crested	*Melampyrum cristatum*	61,68
Field	*Melampyrum arvense*	62
Cowbane	*Cicuta virosa*	82,83
Cowslip	*Primula veris*	16,18,*34*,50,51, 52,73
Cowslop	*Primula veris*	16
Cranesbill, Blood-red	*Geranium sanguineum*	23
Bloody	*Geranium sanguineum*	23
Crocus, Autumn	*Crosus nudiflorus*	17
Saffron	*Croscus sativus*	17
Crowcup	*Fritillaria meleagris*	14
Crowfeet	*Lotus corniculatus*	77,85,111
Cuckoo-pint	*Arum maculatum*	73,74
Cudweed, Jersey	*Gnaphalium luteoalbum*	*100*,104
Small	*Filago minima*	124
Cullions	*Orchis mascula*	18
Daffodil, Garden	*Narcissus sp.*	20,29,30
Wild	*Narcissus pseudonarcissus*	29,*41*
Daisy, Ox-eye	*Leucanthemum vulgare*	14,18,*19*,24,26, *34*
Dandelion	*Taraxacum sp.*	31
Dane's-blood	*Pulsatilla vulgaris*	23
Dead-nettle, Red	*Lamium purpureum*	55
Death-bell	*Fritillaria meleagris*	14
Devil's-tongue	*Papaver rhoeas*	31
Dittander	*Lepidum latifolium*	107
Dock, Golden	*Rumex maritimus*	90
Dog-violet, Common	*Viola riviniana*	50,*54*
Early	*Viola reichenbachiana*	50
Dolly, Red	*Papaver rhoeas*	31
Dollycaps	*Aquilegia vulgaris*	83
Earaches	*Papaver rhoeas*	31
Egg-and-cheese	*Oxalis acetosella*	52
Elecampane	*Inula helenium*	21
Elm	*Ulmus sp.*	57,63,74

137

Species	Scientific name	
Equality, Herb of	*Paris quadrifolia*	56
Everlasting-pea, Norfolk	*Lathyrus heterophyllus*	105
Eyebright	*Euphrasia sp.*	21
Fair-maids-of-France	*Saxifraga granulata*	24
Fennel, Hogs'	*Peucedanum officinale*	106,107
Feverwort	*Centaurium erythraea*	104
Figwort, Common	*Scrophularia nodosa*	60
Green	*Scrophularia umbrosa*	60
Yellow	*Scrophularia vernalis*	60,69
Finger, Bloody-man's	*Orchis morio*	18
Fingers, Five	*Lotus corniculatus*	111
Fingers-and-toes	*Lotus corniculatus*	111
Fireweed	*Chamerion angustifolia*	103
Fishleaves	*Alisma plantago-aquatica*	85
Flag, Yellow	*Iris pseudacorus*	74,92
Flannel-flower	*Verbascum thapsus*	29
-jacket	*Verbascum thapsus*	29
Flax, Fairy	*Linum catharticum*	21
Narrow-leaved	*Linium bienne*	105
Pale	*Linium bienne*	105
Purging	*Linum catharticum*	21
Fleabane, Canadian	*Conyza canadensis*	31
Fleaweed	*Galium verum*	24
Fligger	*Iris pseudacorus*	74
Flower, Dane's	*Pulsatilla vulgaris*	23
Guinea-hen	*Fritillaria meleagris*	14
Queen Anne's	*Narcissus pseudonarcissus*	29
Fluff, White	*Menyanthes trifoliata*	90
Forget-me-not, Water	*Myosotis scorpiodes*	77
Foxglove	*Digitalis purpurea*	59
Fritillary, Snakeshead	*Fritillaria meleagris*	14,15,16,17,18, 19
Frog-cups	*Fritillaria meleagris*	14
Frogbit	*Hydrocharis morsus-ranae*	85,95,96
Fumitory, Dense-flowered	*Fumaria densiflora*	130
Fine-leaved	*Fumaria parviflora*	130
Garlic, Wild	*Allium ursinum*	50,53,55
Wood	*Allium ursinum*	53
Gentian, Autumn	*Gentianella amarella*	21
Marsh	*Gentiana pneumonanthe*	84,88
Spring	*Gentiana verna*	88
Geum, Hybrid	*Geum X intermedium*	56
Glasswort	*Salicornia sp.*	107,108
Gold	*Chrysanthemum segetum*	30
Goosefoot, Stinking	*Chenopodium vulvaria*	106
Goosey-gander	*Orchis morio*	18
Gorse	*Ulex europaeus*	87
Grape hyacinth, Garden	*Muscari armeniacum*	53,123
Wild	*Muscari neglectum*	53,122,123,124, 127
Grape, Oregon	*Mahonia aquifolium*	122
Green-weed	*Genista tinctoria*	20
Greening-weed	*Genista tinctoria*	20
Greenweed, Dyer's	*Genista tinctoria*	*12*,20
Ground-pine	*Ajuga chamaepitys*	129
Halfpennies-and-pennies	*Hydrocharis morsus-ranae*	85
Hare's-ear, Slender	*Bupleurum tenuissimum*	107
Harebell	*Campanula rotundifolia*	53
Hazel	*Corylus avellana*	56,57,58,63
Headache	*Papaver rhoeas*	73
Heartsease	*Viola tricolor*	130
Heath, Cross-leaved	*Erica tetralix*	87,104
Heather	*Calluna vulgaris*	87,104,119
Bell,	*Erica cinerea*	87,104
Hedge-parsley, Knotted	*Torilis nodosa*	107
Hellebore, Green	*Helleborus viridis*	62
Stinking	*Helleborus foetidus*	62,63,*70*
Helleborine, Broad-leaved	*Epipactis helleborine*	47,57,58,131
Green-flowered	*Epipactis phyllanthes*	131,*134*
Marsh	*Epipactis palustris*	79,*93*
Violet	*Epipactis purpurata*	47,57,69
Hens-and-chickens	*Aquilegia vulgaris*	83
Herb, Pair	*Paris quadrifolia*	56
Herb-bennet	*Geum urbanum*	55
-Peter	*Primula veris*	16
Hogweed	*Heracleum sphondylium*	26
Hop	*Humulus lupulus*	77
Hornbeam	*Carpinus betulus*	46,58
Horned-poppy, Yellow	*Glaucium flavum*	103,104,*114*
Horseradish	*Armoracia rusticana*	53,107
Hyacinth, Starch	*Muscari neglectum*	53,123
Iris, Stinking	*Iris foetidissima*	62
Yellow	*Iris pseudacorus*	74,*91*

Species	Scientific name	
Jack, Ragged -behind-the-garden-gate	*Silene flos-cuculi* *Viola tricolor*	73 130
Jacks, Naked	*Colchium autumnale*	17
Kale, Sea	*Crambe maritima*	105,106,109, *114*
Keeslip	*Galium verum*	16
Kingcup	*Caltha palustris*	74
Kiss-at-the-garden-gate -me-over-the-garden gate	*Viola tricolor* *Viola tricolor*	130 129
Knawel, Annual	*Scleranthus annuus*	128
Perennial	*Scleranthus perennis*	123,128
Ladder-to-heaven	*Convallaria majalis*	59
Ladies'-fingers	*Primula vulgaris x Primula veris*	21,*51*
Ladies, Butterfly	*Papaver rhoeas*	31
Naked	*Colchium autumnale*	17
Lady's-candle	*Verbascum thapsus*	29
-smock	*Cardamine pratensis*	16,73,74,*91*
-tresses, Autumn	*Spiranthes spiralis*	20,25,*39*
Creeping	*Goodyera repens*	25,60,61
Land-whin	*Ononis repens*	111
Lazarus-bell	*Fritillaria meleagris*	14
Lettuce, Least	*Lactuca saligna*	90
Lichens, Cladonia	*Cladonia sp.*	*133*
Lightning	*Papaver rhoeas*	31
Lily, Chequered	*Fritillaria meleagris*	14
Lent	*Narcissus pseudonarcissus*	29
Leopard's	*Fritillaria meleagris*	14
May	*Maianthemum bifolium*	54,59,60
Pheasant's	*Fritillaria meleagris*	14
Snakeshead	*Fritillaria meleagris*	14
Woolpit	*Convallaria majalis*	59
-convall	*Convallaria majalis*	59
-of-the-valley	*Convallaria majalis*	54,59,85
Lime, small-leaved	*Tilia cordata*	46,47,58,63
Ling	*Calluna vulgaris*	87,104,*113*
Linseed	*Linum usitatissimum*	31,*43*
Liriconfancy	*Convallaria majalis*	59
Loosestrife, Purple	*Lythrum salicaria*	73,74,80
Yellow	*Lysimachia vulgaris*	73,74,80,*91*
Lords-and-ladies	*Arum maculatum*	74
Lousewort	*Pedicularis sylvatica*	62,87
Marsh	*Pedicularis palustris*	80
Lucerne	*Medicago sativa ssp. sativa*	125
Sand	*Medicago sativa ssp. varia*	125
Luck	*Anthyllis vulneraria*	21
Lupin, Tree	*Lupinus arboreus*	105
Mallow, Marsh	*Althaea officinalis*	111,*116*
Maple, Field	*Acer campestre*	46,63
Marigold, Corn	*Chrysanthemum segetum*	*12*,30,31
Marsh	*Caltha palustris*	74,*81*
Marjoram	*Origanum vulgare*	22
Marram	*Ammophila arenaria*	101,102
Mary's-buds	*Caltha palustris*	74
Masslin	*Viscum album*	63
May blobs	*Caltha palustris*	73,74
Meadowsweet	*Filipendula ulmaria*	73,74,80
Medick, Bur	*Medicago minima*	124,125,*135*
Hybrid wild	*Medicago sativa ssp. varia*	125
Purple	*Medicago sativa ssp. sativa*	125
Sickle	*Medicago sativa ssp. falcata*	125,*134*
Small	*Medicago minima*	125
Yellow	*Medicago sativa ssp. falcata*	125
Men, Naked	*Colchium autumnale*	17
Mercury, Dog's	*Mercurialis perennis*	47,48
Mezerion	*Daphne mezereum*	130
Milk-vetch, Purple	*Astragalus danicus*	125
Milkmaids	*Cardamine pratensis*	73
Milkwort, Common	*Polygala vulgaris*	22
Sea	*Glaux maritima*	105
Mint, Whorled	*Mentha arvensis x M. aquatica*	91
Mislin-bush	*Viscum album*	63
Mistletoe	*Viscum album*	63,*70*
Moschatel	*Adoxa moschatellina*	52,66
Mugwort	*Artemisia vulgaris*	126
Mullein, Great	*Verbascum thapsus*	29
Hoary	*Verbascum pulverulentum*	29,*42*
White	*Verbascum lychnitis*	105
Mustard, Tower	*Arabis glabra*	130
Nannies, Naked	*Colchium autumnale*	17

138

Species	Scientific name		Species	Scientific name	
Nightshade, Enchanter's	*Circaea lutetiana*	47	Field	*Papaver rhoeas*	31
Woody	*Solanum dulcamara*	77	Poison	*Papaver rhoeas*	31
Oak	*Quercus robar*	46,47,55,58,62, 63,75,120	Sea	*Glaucium flavum*	106
One-berry	*Paris quadrifolia*	56	Primrose	*Primula vulgaris*	24,50,51,*54*,86, 105
Orache, Frosted	*Atriplex laciniata*	102	Purple, Long	*Orchis mascula*	18
Long-stalked	*Atriplex longipes*	102	Purslane, Sea	*Halimione portulacoides*	108,*115*
Mealy	*Atriplex laciniata*	102	Ragged-Robin	*Lychnis flos-cuculi*	73,92
Orchid, Bee	*Ophrys apifera*	26,27,*42*	Ragwort	*Senecio jacobaea*	31,103
Bird's-nest	*Neottia nidus-avis*	56	Ramsden	*Allium ursinum*	53
Bog	*Hammarbya paludosa*	80	Ramsons	*Allium ursinum*	48,53,55,66
Burnt	*Orchis ustulata*	21	Rape, Oilseed	*Brassica napus* ssp. *oleifera*	31,*42*
Common Spotted	*Dactylorhiza fuchsii*	27,28,39,77	Rassals	*Ononis repens*	111
Early marsh	*Dactylorhiza incarnata*	77,78,*84*	Rattle, Red	*Pedicularis palustris*	80
spider	*Ophrys sphegodes*	21,131	Yellow	*Rhinanthus minor*	18,*33*
-purple	*Orchis mascula*	18,35,50,74	-basket	*Rhinanthus minor*	18
Fen	*Liparis loeselii*	79,80,85	Rest-harrow	*Ononis repens*	22,23,105,111
Field butterfly	*Platanthera bifolia*	58,59	Robin, Red	*Orchis mascula*	18
Fly	*Ophrys insectifera*	27	Rock-rose, Common	*Helianthemum nummularium*	20,21,36
Fragrant	*Gymnadenia conopsea* ssp. *conopsea*	79	Rocket, Sea	*Cakile maritima*	102
Frog	*Coeloglossum viride*	20,35	Rose, Canker	*Papaver rhoeas*	31
Greater butterfly	*Platanthera chlorantha*	58	Corn	*Pavaver rhoeas*	31
Green Man	*Aceras anthropophorum*	28	Rupturewort	*Herniaria glabra*	123
Green-veined	*Orchis morio*	18	Ryegrass, Perennial	*Loilium perenne*	13
-winged	*Orchis morio*	18,20,35	Saffron, Meadow	*Colchium autumnale*	17,*19*
Heath spotted	*Dactylorhiza maculata*	27,28,87	Sainfoin	*Onobrychis viciifolia*	14,22,37
Irish marsh	*Dactylorhiza traunsteineri*	78	Sallow	*Salix* sp.	75
Leopard marsh	*Dactylorhiza praetermissa* var. *junialis*	78	Saltwort, Black	*Glaux maritima*	105
Lesser butterfly	*Platanthera bifolia*	58,59	Prickly	*Salsola kali*	102
Lizard	*Himantoglossum hircinum*	23,24,37	Samphire	*Salicornia* sp.	108
Man	*Aceras anthropophorum*	20,28,39,131	Golden	*Inula crithmoides*	108
Marsh fragrant	*Gymnadenia conopsea* ssp. *densiflora*	77,78,79,*94*	Marsh	*Salicornia* sp.	106,107,*110*
Military	*Orchis militaris*	22,*127*,130	Rock	*Crithmum maritimum*	108
Narrow-leaved marsh	*Dactylorhiza traunsteineri*	78	Sandwort, Sea	*Honckenya peploides*	105
Pugsley's marsh	*Dactylorhiza traunsteineri*	78	Sanicle	*Sanicula europaea*	55
Pyramidal	*Anacamptis pyramidalis*	19,28,*40*,79	Saxifrage, Meadow	*Saxifraga granulata*	24,25,*38*,128
Scented	*Gymnadenia conopsea*	79	Pepper	*Silaum silaus*	16
Soldier	*Orchis militaris*	130	Scabious, Devilsbit	*Succisia pratensis*	80,82
Southern marsh	*Dactylorhiza praetermissa*	77,78,79	Small	*Scabiosa columbaria*	21
Traunsteiner's	*Dactylorhiza traunsteineri*	78	Scurvy-grass, Common	*Cochlearia officinalis*	108,109
Wasp	*Ophrys apifera* var. *trollii*	27	Danish	*Cochlearia danica*	26
Western marsh	*Dactylorhiza majalis*	79	Early	*Cochlearia danica*	26
Wood butterfly	*Platanthera chlorantha*	59	Sea-heath	*Frankenia laevis*	103,109,*116*
Oxlip	*Primula elatior*	50,51,*54*	-holly	*Eryngium maritimum*	102,103,*112*
False	*Primula vulgaris* x *Primula veris*	50,51,*64*	-lavender, Common	*Limonium vulgare*	107,108,*115*
Paigle	*Primula veris*	16	Matted	*Limonium bellidifolium*	109,*116*
Palsy-wort	*Primula veris*	16	Rock	*Limonium binervosum*	109,*114*
Pansy, Breckland	*Viola tricolor* ssp. *curtisii*	129	-pink	*Armeria maritima*	109
Wild	*Viola tricolor*	129	-spurrey, Greater	*Spergularia media*	109
Paris, Herb	*Paris quadrifolia*	56,57	Seablite, Shrubby	*Suaeda vera*	103,109,*117*
Parnassus, Grass of	*Parnassia palustris*	80,82,*94*	Serpent's-tongue	*Sagittaria sagittifolia*	85
Parsley, Cow	*Anthriscus sylvestris*	26	Shamrock	*Oxalis acetosella*	52
Milk	*Peucedanum palustre*	83	Sheepsbit	*Jasione montana*	102,105
Pasque-flower	*Pulsatilla vulgaris*	23,37	Shoes, Ladies'	*Aquilegia vulgaris*	83
Passeflower	*Pulsatilla vulgaris*	23	Snowdrop	*Galanthus nivalis*	49,50,55,*71*
Pea, Marsh	*Lathyrus palustris*	72,82	Soldiers	*Papaver rhoeas*	74
Sea	*Lathyrus japonicus*	104,105,106, 109,*110*	Red	*Papaver rhoeas*	31
Pearlwort, Knotted	*Sagina nodosa*	91	Southernwood, Field	*Artemisia compestris*	126
Peggle	*Primula veris*	16	Sea	*Seriphidium maritima*	109
Penny-weed	*Hydrocharis morsus-ranae*	85	Sow-thistle, Corn	*Sonchus arvensis*	87
Peril, Picnicker's	*Cirsium acaule*	21	Marsh	*Sonchus palustris*	84,86,87
Petticoat, Red	*Papaver rhoeas*	31	Perennial	*Sonchus arvensis*	*84*,87
Pickerel-weed	*Stratiotes aloides*	85	Spearwort, Greater	*Ranunculus lingua*	86,97
Pig's-eyes	*Cardamine pratensis*	73	Speedwell, Breckland	*Veronica praecox*	120,121,123, *132*
-foot	*Lotus corniculatus*	111	Fingered	*Veronica triphyllos*	120,121,*132*
Pimpernel, Bog	*Anagallis tenella*	88,96	Spiked	*Veronica spicata* ssp. *spicata*	14,22,121,*127*
Pincushion	*Centaurea cyanus*	30	Spring	*Veronica verna*	121,122
Pine, Corsican	*Pinus nigra* ssp. *laricio*	60,123	Wall	*Veronica arvensis*	121
Scots	*Pinus sylvestris*	60,62,120,123	Western Spiked	*Veronica spicata* ssp. *hybrida*	121
Pink, Maiden	*Dianthus deltoides*	*118*,128	Spurge, Cypress	*Euphorbia cyparissias*	122
Proliferous	*Petrorhagia prolifera*	17,128	Sea	*Euphorbia paralias*	103
Pintle, Priest's	*Orchis mascula*	18	Wood	*Euphorbia amygdaliodes*	51,65,*127*
Plant, Bread-and-cheese	*Oxalis acetosella*	52	Squinancywort	*Asperula cynanchica*	20,21,36
Ploughman's spikenard	*Inula conyza*	21,104	St Peter's-keys-of-heaven	*Primula veris*	16
Poplar	*Populus* sp.	56	Star-of-Bethlehem, Common	*Ornithogalum angustifollium*	124,*132*
Popple	*Agrostemma githago*	30	Yellow	*Gagea lutea*	44,48,49
Poppy, Common	*Papaver rhoeas*	2,30,31,32,73	Stitchwort	*Stellaria holostea*	48,55
Corn	*Papaver rhoeas*	31	Stonecrop, Biting	*Sedum acre*	103
			English	*Sedum anglicum*	103
			Mossy	*Crassula tillaea*	131,*135*
			Storksbill, Common	*Erodium cicutarium*	103

Species	Scientific name		Species	Scientific name	
Sulphurweed	*Peucedanum officinale*	106.107	Marsh	*Valeriana dioica*	80
Sundew, Common	*Drosera rotundifolia*	88,89,*98*	Vetch, Kidney	*Anthyllis vulneraria*	14,21,*36*,51
Great	*Drosera longifolia*	88,89	Yellow	*Vicia lutea*	105,*113*
Long-leaved	*Drosera longifolia*	88	Violet, Bog	*Pinguicula vulgaris*	89
Oblong-leaved	*Drosera intermedia*	88,89	Horse	*Viola riviniana*	50
Round-leaved	*Drosera rotundifolia*	88	Sweet	*Viola odorata*	50
Sweethearts	*Listera ovata*	57	Wallflower	*Erysimum cheiri*	101
Sympathy, Plant of	*Armeria maritima*	109	Water-dropwort, Narrow-		
Taper, Hag's	*Verbascum thapsus*	29	leaved	*Oenanthe silaifolia*	90
High	*Verbascum thapsus*	29	-lily, Fringed	*Nymphoides peltata*	73,90
King's	*Verbascum thapsus*	29	White	*Nymphaea alba*	73,74
Lady's	*Verbascum thapsus*	29	Yellow	*Nuphar lutea*	73,74,75,*92*
Tears, Our Lady's	*Convallaria majalis*	59	-pepper, Small	*Persicaria minor*	90
Thistle, Carline	*Carlina vulgaris*	104	-plantain	*Alisma plantago-aquatica*	85
Dwarf	*Cirsium acaule*	21	-soldier	*Stratiotes aloides*	85,86,95
Marsh	*Cirsium palustre*	80,*94*	-violet	*Hottonia palustris*	86,96
Meadow	*Cirsium dissectum*	80,*93*	Weasel-snout	*Lamiastrum galeobdolon*	55
Slender	*Cirsium tenuiflorus*	107	Weed, Red	*Papaver rhoeas*	31
Stemless	*Cirsium acaule*	21	Welcome-to-our-house	*Euphorbia cyparissias*	122
Thrift	*Armeria maritima*	109,*117*	Whin, Petty	*Genista anglica*	87
Thunder-cup	*Papaver rhoeas*	31	Whore, Naked	*Colchicum autumnale*	17
Thunderbolt	*Papaver rhoeas*	31	Widow, Rampant	*Orchis mascula*	18
Thunderflower	*Papaver rhoeas*	31	Willowherb, Great	*Epilobium hirsutum*	26
Thyme	*Thymus sp.*	20,36,126	Rosebay	*Chamerion angustifolium*	103
Breckland	*Thymus serpyllum*	*118*,126	Windflower	*Anemone nemorosa*	52
Greater	*Thymus pulegioides*	126	Wintergreen, Round-		
Large	*Thymus pulegioides*	126	leaved	*Pyrola rotundifolia*	83,85,*94*
Wild	*Thymus polytrichus*	22,126	Woad	*Isatis tinctoria*	20
Tillea, Mossy	*Crassula tillaea*	131	Wood-sorrel	*Oxalis acetosella*	52,66
Toads-heads	*Fritillaria meleagris*	14	Woodruff, Sweet	*Galium odoratum*	55,68
Torches	*Verbascum thapsus*	29	Wormwood, Bitter	*Artemisia absinthium*	126
Trefoil, Birds-foot	*Lotus corniculatus*	14,*19*,51,111	Field	*Artemisia campestris*	125,*134*
Water	*Menyanthes trifoliata*	90	Sea	*Seriphidium maritimum*	109
Twayblade	*Listera ovata*	57,130	Yellow-wort	*Blackstonia perfoliata*	22
Valerian	*Valeriana officinalis*	80,*93*			

General Index

All figures in *italics* refer to illustrations.
EWT Essex Wildlife Trust Reserve
NWT Norfolk Wildlife Trust Reserve
SWT Suffolk Wildlife Trust Reserve
NNR National Nature Reserve

Acle....87
Akeroyd, John....128
Alburgh....28
Alde, River....101
Aldeburgh....101
Ant Valley....80,87
arable....10 *et seq*,61,101,111,120 *et seq*
Ardleigh....60
Ashbocking....17
Asheldham Pits....27
Ashwellthorpe Lower Wood (NWT)..47,51,57
assembly rules....48
Ballingdon....131
banks....74 *et seq*,105,107,120,123,124
Barnby Broad....76,78,88
Barnhamcross Common....129
Barton Broad NNR (NWT)....75
Bath Hills, Ditchingham....62
Bawdsey Haven....101
Beachamwell Fen....21
Beaulieu....106
Beccles....29,85
Beckett, Gillian....128
Beeston Bog....78,79,89
Regis....25,124
Belchamp St Paul....131
Water....78
Benacre Broad....76,105
Ness....102,105
NNR....30,105
Black Ditches....22
Blackwater Estuary NNR....101
River....8,90,108
Blakeney Point (National Trust)....104,105, 106,109,*110*
Blakes Wood, Danbury (EWT)....57
Blickling Estate (National Trust)....55
Blyth, River....101
Blythburgh....87,101,109
Bodham....60
bogs....73 *et seq*
Bonny Wood, Stowmarket (SWT)....47
Booton Common (NWT)....57,79,88,89
borrow-pits....21
Botanical Society of the British Isles....10,14
Boyton Marshes....102
Bradfield Woods NNR (SWT)....47,51
Bradwell Shell Bank (EWT)....106
-on-Sea....8,101
Brandon....23,58,119,126
Breck, Breckland....8,16,21,25,26,28,31,52, 58,60,61,107,119 *et seq*
Brightwell....78
Briston....105
Broadfield Wood....56
Broadland, the Broads....73 *et seq*,102,119
Broads Authority....75
Brooke....59
Bryants Heath, Felmingham....80
Bull, Alec....83,129
Bulls Wood, Lavenham (SWT)....47
Bure, River....76,82,87
Burgh Common (NWT)....82,85,86
Burnham Overy Staithe....79,109
Bury St Edmunds....21,22,23,29,60,119
Butcher's Marsh (SWT)....78
Butt Plantation, Mildenhall Woods....130
Buxton....55
Heath....79,82,*84*,88,89
calcicoles....119
calcifuges....119
Caldecote Fen....21,25,83
Calthorpe Broad....75
Camps Heath Marshes (SWT)....78
Carlton Marshes (SWT)....85
carr woodland....75,77
Castle Marshes (SWT)....85
Rising....48
Castor Hanglands NNR....62
Catfield Dyke....82
Cavenham....22
Heath NNR....22,23
Cawston....60
chalk....8 *passim*
grassland....21,22,27,28,83
Chalkney Wood....56,58
Cherry Hill/Herringswell Road....122
Chet, River....87
Chigborough Lakes (EWT)....78,85,90
Chippenhall Green....20
churchyards....*19*,24,25,29,30,49,60,112
Clacton....101,109
Clarke, W.G.....122,124
Cley....104,105,106,109,*114*
Cockfield....50
Cockshoot Broad (NWT)....75,82
Colchester....18,29,103,107
Colchis, Georgia....17
Colne Estuary NNR....101
Point (EWT)....101,103,108,109
Combs Wood, Stowmarket (SWT)....47,58
commons....18,27
Coney Weston Fen (SWT)....78
Cookley....27
coppice, coppicing....45,46,56,61
Cornard Mere (SWT)....76,90
Corton....101
Countryside Commission....10,75
County Wildlife Sites....102
Covehithe....101,102
Broad....76
Crabknowe Spit....101
Cranwich....22,60,128
Cringleford....29
Cromer....102
Croxton....90
Cummings, Dr Ian....60
Darsham Marshes (SWT)....78
Deben Estuary....101
River....15
Debenham....15
Decoy Ponds, Bixley Heath....76
Dedham....60
Dengie Marshes....101
Denton....28
Dersingham Bog....89
Devil's Ditch, Cambs....22,23,28,79
Punchbowl....90
Dickleburgh Pightle (NWT)....50
Ditton Green....22
Dovercourt....101,105
dunes....20 *et seq*,60,77,79,82,85,101 *et seq*,119
Dunwich....76,101,102
Common....60
Gap....101
Durham....59
dykes....73 *et seq*,107
East Harling....22,119
Lane....101
Walton Common....21
Winch Common (NWT)....88
Wretham Heath (NWT)....90
Eastbridge, Minsmere....78
Easton Bavents....102
Broad....76
Eccles....60
Eliot, T.S.....128
Ellis, E.A.....80,90,105
Ellough....27
Elveden Farms Ltd....124
Emily's Wood....60
English Nature....9,10,80,102,121,122
Environmentally Sensitive Areas....76
epiphytes....79
Essex Wildlife Trust....9 *passim*
estuaries....76 *et seq*,101 *et seq*
Farming & Wildlife Advisory Groups....10
Felbrigg....59
Felixstowe....101,106,108
Felthorpe....80
Feltwell....129
fens....73 *et seq*
field margins and headlands....13 *passim*
Filby Broad....82
Fingringhoe Wick (EWT)....87
First Church Meadow (SWT)....17
Flixton....62
Decoy....76
Flora of Norfolk....21,131
Forestry Commission....10,58,123,130
Fornham St Genevieve....60
Foulden Common....21,25,78
Fowlmere....90
Fox Fritillary Meadow (SWT)....15
Mrs Queenie....15
Foxburrow Wood (SWT)....57
Foxhole Heath....119,124,125
Foxley Wood (NWT)....47,51
Framlingham Mere (SWT)....76
Framsden....15
Frinton....25,101
Fritton Lake....76
Gage, Sir Thomas....49
Garboldisham....22
Garnham family....20
Gerard, John....23,30,73,103
Gestingthorpe....57
grassland....13 *et seq*,51,107,119 *et seq*
Gray, Thomas....119
Great Blakenham....27
Glenham....48
Hockham Hills and Holes....129
Oakley....108
Ouse, River....90
Whelnetham....62
Yarmouth....103
green lanes....26
greens....27
Griston....48,59
Groton Wood, Sudbury (SWT)....47,58
Gun Hill, Burnham Overy Staithe....103,109, *110*
Gunton....101
Hadleigh....28
Halstead....8
Hamford Water NNR....101,106
Happisburgh....102
Hargrave....62
Harleston....15,123
Harwich....106
Hasketon....20
Haughley Junction....22
Hayley Wood....62
haymaking....15
Heacham....129
heathland....10,14,73 *et seq*,107,119 *et seq*
hectads....9
hedgerows....61,62,63,120,123,129
Hereward the Wake....73
Hethel....27,30,*41*,57
Hickling Broad NNR (NWT)....82
High House, Monewden (SWT)...17,*19*,20,28
Higham....22
Hitchcock's Meadow, Danbury (EWT)....20
Hockering Wood (NWT)....52
Holkham....59,60,104,105
Gap....109,111
Hollesley....109,131
Holme Dunes NNR (NWT)....28,77,78,104
Holt....15,60
Country Park....25,57,60
Lowes (NWT)....57,78,82,88,89
Honeypot Wood (NWT)....18,47,58,59
Hopkins, Gerard Manley....73
Hopton....79,101
Horningtoft....55,57,58,59
How Hill....*84*,87
Howland Marsh, St Osyth (EWT)....108
Hunstanton....101
Icklingham....22,23,128

Triangle 125
Iken 87,131
Ilketshals, The 28
Ipswich 107
Iron Latch Meadow (EWT) 18
Isle of Dogs 129
Kessingland 102,104,105,108
King's Lynn 59,83
Lakenheath 24,77,119,120,121,123,124, *127*
Poors Fen (SWT) 78,82
Lambs Common 21
Landguard Common (SWT) 102,104,105, 106,*114*,124
Lang, David 58
Langmere 90
Lavenham 28
Lawford 60
Linnaeus 62
Little Baddow Heath, Danbury (EWT) 58
Blakenham 28
Cressingham 129
Lolly Moor (NWT) 57,78,79
Loshes Meadows (EWT) 78
Lothingland 77,85,86,87
Lowestoft 29,57,76,85,102
Ludham Marshes NNR 85,86
Mabey, Richard 15,32,52
Maidscross Hill 121,124
Manningtree 111,125
Marham Fen 21
Market Weston Fen (SWT) 78,79,82,89
marshes ....15,27,73 *et seq*,101 *et seq*,121
Martham South Broad NNR 75
Martin's Meadow, Monewden (SWT) 15,17, 18,20,28
meadows ....13 *et seq*,73 *et seq*,107
meres ....73 *et seq*
Mersea 101
Island 109
Merton 129
Mickfield 16
Meadow (SWT) 15,16,17,18,*19*,20,51
Middle Wood, Ofton 58
Middleton 85
Mildenhall 20,22,25,77,78,119,130
Ministry of Agriculture 10,61
Minsmere 78,87,101,102
Montagu family 106
Mundesley 111
Mundford 58
Narborough Railway Line (SWT) 21,22, 28,57,78
National Nature Reserves 9,10,101,102, 104,105
Rivers Authority 10,77
Seed Bank 14
Trust 9,10,55,102,104
Naze, The 106
Nedging 28
Newbourne Springs, Ipswich (SWT) 57
Newmarket 21
Heath 21,22,79
Norfolk Wildlife Trust ....9 *passim*
North Cove (SWT) 78,88
Denes, Great Yarmouth 102
Lopham 26
-East Essex Flora Project 76
Northfield Wood, Onehouse 59
Norwich 29,30,83,86,120
Nunnery, Thetford 129
Old Racecourse, Holt 60
Ore, River 101,109
Orford Ness 101,102
Orwell, River 101
Osea Island 109
Oulton Broad 76,78,82
Marshes (SWT) 82,86,88
Ouse Washes ....73 *et seq*
Overstrand 78
Oxley Meadow (EWT) 20
Pakefield 101,105,108
Cliffs 104,105,111
Parham 27
Parkeston 29
pastures 15,20
peat 8
pebble beds 101
Pentlow 21
Petch, Dr C.P. & Swann, E.L. 21,30,59,83, 105,106
pingos 86
plantlife 10,129
pollards and pollarding 46,61
ponds ....76 *et seq*
Potter Heigham 87
Potts, James 48
Priestly Wood, Needham Market 58
Rackham, Oliver 13,47,61
Ramparts Field 128
Ransome, Arthur 106
Ranworth Broad (NWT) 82
Rattlesden 27
Rawhall 58,62
Ray Island (EWT) 108
Raydon 57
Reach 22
red crag 101
Redgrave & Lopham Fen NNR (SWT) 57, 78,79,82,89
Reepham 87,88,89
Rex Graham Reserve, Mildenhall (SWT) ...57, 130
Ringmere 90,*99*
Ringstead Downs (NWT) 20,25
Risby 22
Roads, A11 29,119,123
A140 15
A1101 125
B1112 124,125
Roydon Common NNR (NWT) ...59,82,86,89
run-off 16,26,55,75,87
Rushmere, Ipswich 76
Saffrom Walden 17
Sainsbury Orchid Project 80
saltings 101,105,107,108
saltmarshes ....73 *et seq*,101 *et seq*
sand ....8,101 *et seq*,119,*133*
-blows 119
Sandlings 123,129
Santon 58
Downham 58,119
Sapiston 26
Saxmundham 48
Scarce Plants in Britain 62,85,106,129
Scarning Fen (NWT) 57,79,82,83,89
Scolt Head Island NNR (NWT) 104
Scrubs Wood, Danbury (EWT) 58
sea cliffs ....22,101 *et seq*,121
walls 101,107,125
Secret Water 106
Semer 26
set-aside 10,13,14,31
Shakespeare, William 18,45,73,74,101, 103,108
shellbanks 101
Sheringham 59,78,111,124
shingle bars 101,102,104,105,106,108
Shingle Street 76,101,105,106,108,*110*
Shotesham 38
Shotley 108
Sidestrand 78
Simpson, F.W. 20,23,50,52,56,63,89,109, 121,122,123,131
Simpson's Flora of Suffolk 131
Saltings (SWT) 109
Sites of Special Scientific Interest 10,58, 102,128
Sizewell 77,101,102
Skipper's Island (EWT) 106
Smallburgh Fen (NWT) 79,82
Snape 87,111
Warren 101
Snetterton 60
Snettisham 106
Gravel Pit 128
South Elmhams, The 28
Southminster 27
Southwold 57,76,101
Species Recovery Programme 80
Sprats Water, Carlton Marshes (SWT) 86
Stanford Training Area 123
Stansgate 108
Staverton Park 46
Stetchworth 22
Stiffkey 60
Stoke Holy Cross 30
Stokesby 87
Stone Point 101
Stour Estuary 101
Wood 52
River 28,108,111
Strumpshaw 26,82
Stuston Common (SWT) 60
Sudbury 21,47,76,90
Suffolk Orchid Survey 20,57,58,77
Wildlife Trust ....9 *passim*
Surlingham 87
Swaffham 119
Swanton Great Wood 48,51,*54*,59
Novers 59,60
Tarpey, Terri & Heath, Jerry 55,58,106
tetrads 9
Thelnetham Fen (SWT) 79,82,89
Thelveton 18
Therfield Heath 22
Thetford 126
by-pass 26
Forest 123
Heath NNR (NWT) 121,126,128
Warren Lodge 126
Thompson Common (NWT) 77,*84*,86
Thorpeness 103,124
Thurne 87
Broads 75,82
River 87,*91*
Thursford Wood (NWT) 47
Topcroft *19*,26,28
Trimley 108,109
Tuddenham Gallops (SWT) ..121,122,123,*127*
Tulip Hills, Lexham 23
Tunstall 87
Upton Broad 75
Fen (NWT) 59,77,79,82,85
verges, roadside ....14 *et seq*,55,62,82,105, 121 *et seq*
Walberswick 101,102,108,109
Walsey Hills, Cley 128
Walsingham, Lord 48,129
Walton 101
Wangford Warren (SWT) 119,*133*
Warham Camp 22,28
Wash, The 73,102,106,109,111,130,131
Watch House, Blakeney Point 106
water pollution and eutrophication ...75 *et seq*, 107
Water Wood, Butley 30
Waterhall Meadows, Danbury (EWT) 25
Wattisham 26,28
Waveney/Little Ouse Valley 62,77,79,87,89
Wayland Wood (NWT) 47,48,52,*54*
weeds, arable 123,129
Weeting 22,58,122
Castle 129
Heath NNR (NWT) 14,121,122,*127*,128
Wells 22,28,59,60,85,102
Welnetham 28
West Stow 128,129
Westleton 59,131
Westwick 60
wet heaths ....73 *et seq*
Weybourne 102
Wickham Bishops 62
Wild Flower Society 10
Wildflower Seeds Working Group 14
Wildlife & Countryside Act, 1981 86,123
Winks Meadow, Metfield (SWT) ..20,25,28,*34*
Winterton Dunes NNR 85,102,104,*113*
Witham 62
Wither, George 13
Wolves Wood 47,58
wood-pasture 46
Woodbastwick 82
Woodham Walter Common, Danbury (EWT) 58
Woodland Trust 9,10
woodland, broadleaved ....45 *et seq*,120
coniferous 45,47,57,60,86,130
secondary 55
Woodton 26
Wortham 57
Wretham 90
Yare, River 87
Yeats, W.B. 10

Subscribers

Presentation Copies

1 Norfolk Wildlife Trust
2 Suffolk Wildlife Trust
3 Norwich & Norfolk Naturalists' Society
4 Norfolk Library Authority
5 Suffolk Library Authority
6 Essex Library Authority

7 Dr & Mrs Stephen Martin
8 Clive & Carolyn Birch
9 Angela M.B. Martin
10 Richard Edward Martin
11 Anna Elizabeth Martin
12 Valerie Purton
13 Peter Mangold
14 Ray Hammond
15 D.S. Martin
16 R.W. Woods
17 S.J. Martin
18 Ron Kerridge
19 Jennifer Green
20 Tony & Paulina Powell
21-22 Ian Cummings
23 Gale Carruthers
24 Alan R. Folkes
25 Harriet Cooper
26 Alan Berry
27 Pat & Dick Waddington
28-29 Mrs S. Metters
30 James M. Clayton
31 Robert Smedley
32 Valerie Grogutt
33 Carol & Paul
34 P.M.S. Gillam
35 F.D. Kelsey
36 Maureen Leveton
37 Jean & John Timbers
38 Paul G.L. Williams
39 Michael R. Hall
40 Marguerite Chappell
41 R.A. Benson
42 M.J. Easton
43 Dr C.G. Smith
44 Mrs V.G. Balfour
45 C.A. Blenkiron
46 R.C. Fiske
47 Rosemary Tilbrook
48 Dr A.G. Moss
49 Martin Collier
50 Bryan Sage
51 Ruth Hadman
52 Mrs A. M. Austin
53 Derek Howlett
54 Simon Burrell
55 J.A. Ashley
56 Mary Dorling
57 Rona Burton
58 Peter J. Wilson
59 M.H. Helliwell
60 Brian J. Sharp
61 D.J. Thurtle
62 T.N.D. Peet
63 Mrs F.R. Wylam
64 Adele Mallen
65 Rex & Barbara Hancy
66 C.N. Arnold
67 Frances Schumann
68 Miss S. Freeman
69 J.N. Rounce
70 R.W. Ellis
71 Alan Cornish & Penny Coventon
72 John Antram
73 Christine West
74 Christopher Mann
75 R.J. Govett
76 Derek K. Stone
77 Stella Bryant
78 P.J. Fairrie
79 Anne Oxenford
80 Mrs M.M. Hogg
81 Margaret Barbara Biggs
82 W.A. Montague
83 Mrs R. Phillips
84 Shiona Hardie
85 J.D. Quinlan
86 Pam Ireland
87 Nathan & Tommy Wood
88 Miles Barne
89 Jean Ramsbottom
90 A.M. Clayton
91 Paul Owen Whittle
92 Christopher Curtis
93 Margaret S. Newstead
94 Carol Joy Wilson
95 T. Illsley
96-97 Mrs A.P. Boyle
98 Dr Stephen Bolt
99 K. Johnson
100 Miss Winifred G. Wearn
101 Mrs Jane Leeds
102 Miss Merle Leeds
103 Bobbie Warren
104 Mrs M.S. Bucknell
105 Glen Sharman
106 James McQuillan
107 William A. Porter
108 J. Platts-Mills
109 B.T. Gooding
110 Mrs D.M. Agnew
111 Frances Bee
112 P.E. Tucker
113 O.D. Green
114 Mrs N.H.A. Cheyne
115-116 P.M.S. Gillam
117 Peter I. Payne
118 Edward Bolger
119 P.E. Tucker
120 F.R. Trevett
121 Ian McClintock
122 Betty Curtis
123 Raymond Frostick
124 Mrs J. Pamela Ellis
125 Stephen Hancock
126 Gill Lister & Family
127 Susan Mealing-Mills
128 R.E. Barker
129 P.T.W. Flower
130 Richard Ball
131 Dr Susan Willmington
132 Mary Fletcher
133 G.R. Newns
134 D.R. Stevens
135 Louise Cooke
136 Mrs Rosemary A. Hanson
137 Mrs Rachel Cubitt
138 M.B. Wainwright
139 Mr Barrie Douglas Harding
140 F.W. Newborn
141 L.A. Lock
142 Percy Sale
143 E. McLernon
144 Mrs W. Bonas
145 P.J. Hodgkins
146 Norman & Kay Sheppard

147 William N. Landells	188 Mrs E. Moynihan	228 Dr F. Marcus Hall
148 Dr J.F.B. Dossetor	189 Jeremy Simpson	229 Jack Smith
149 Mrs Margaret Spink	190 David Ainsley Nadin	230- Mrs P.M. Barnes
150 Mrs A.S. Hankinson	191 Heather Wilson	231
151 Mr & Mrs H.W. Marshall	192 Robyn M. Abel	232 F.R. Lacey
152 John E. Timbers	193 Mr & Mrs John N. Milton	233 Mrs A.C. Gregory
153 Marjorie Betton	194 James Hugh Colledge	234 Sarah Peck
154 Miss M. Martin-Jones	195 J.G. Hilton	235 K.E. Hammond-Kosack
155 Mr & Mrs F. Veltema	196 Liz Ford	236 Stephen Rumsey
156 A.K. Florance	197 E.L. Grant	237 Mrs Eileen Curtis
157 Dr R.S.K. Florance	198 D.H. Cushing	238 Martin & Sabina Gardner
158 Jon Clifton	199 Rosalind J. Weyman	239 Dr Roland E. Randall
159 Susan Downie	200 Anne B. Maconochie	240 Pat & Keith Cavanagh
160 John Austen	201 Jennifer Affleck	241 H.J.B. Birks
161 Aline Spencer Reed	202 Dr Jack Litchfield	242 James Adams
162 B. Blower	203 Dr C.N. Simpson	243 Prof J.G. Duckett
163 Claire & Barry Watkins	204 Mrs Margaret Enger	244 M. Walpole
164 Dr K. Mackenzie	205 Wellsfield Studies Centre (NCC)	245 A. Lyall
165 David & Anna Welti		246 Tanya Barden
166 Michael Densley	206 Mrs J.H. Clarke	247 Bruce Osborne
167 K.M. Whitfield	207 Miss B.G. Cusworth	248 Carol Bennett
168 Kenneth & Gillian Beckett	208 C.D. Bricknell	249 Plant Sciences Library
169 R.G.H. Cant	209 Brian Brookes	250 A. Newton
170 Edward H. Moss	210 T.A. Lording	251 A.R. Perry
171 Sheila Cargil	211 Michael M. Shaw	252 Mark Galliott
172 Dr A.P. Vlasto	212 Mrs Beryl Bailey	253 Mrs E.E. Marper
173 J.W. Dickson	213 Keith Maybury	254 Peter Gateley
174 Patrick J. Keogh	214 A. Johns	255 Monica Hale
175 Miss A.M. Greenway	215 Peter Sell	256 Ray Cleaver
176 Rosemary & Graham Shrive	216 Carol Hawkins	257 K.J. Burrows
177 Eileen Winifred Frewin	217 Brian Laney	258 F.N. Wright
178 Michael & Stella Coates	218 Mark & Clare Kitchen	259 Margaret Knox
179 D.H. Norfolk	219 M. Hardstaff	260 Laurence G. Adams
180 Dr Duncan McKie	220 L.J. Hardstaff	261 Janet M. Adams
181 R.A. Sellwood	221 Mrs Margery Palmer	262 Paul Adam
182 J. Francis	222 K.F. & J.N. Gordon	263 Mrs Kay Gash
183 H.J. Goodhare	223 Dendle French	264 Peter J.B. Hodgkins
184 Sarah Whitcher	224 Rod D'Ayala	265 David N. Robinson
185 Miss Jean Carter	225 David McClinton	
186 P.F. Parmenter	226 Hilli Thompson	*Remaining names unlisted.*
187 J. Riley	227 John Shepperd	

ENDPAPERS: East Anglia – main towns, wildflower sites and other places referred to in the text.

THE WASH
Scolt Head Island
Gun Hill
Holkham
Wells
Blakeney Point
Wolsey Hills
Weybourne
Sheringham
Beeston Bog
Cromer
Overstrand
Sidestrand
Mundesley
Happisburgh
Sutton Broad
Hickling Broad
Horsey Mere
Martham South Broad
Winterton Dunes
North Denes
Great Yarmouth
Holme Dunes
Hunstanton
Heacham
Ringstead Downs
Snettisham
Dersingham
Burnham Overy Staithe
Warham
Stiffkey
R STIFFKEY
R GLAVEN
Holt
Bodham
Hempstead
Felbrigg
Thursford Wood
Swanton Novers,
R BURE
Fulmodeston
Fakenham
BABINGLEY R
Castle Rising
Roydon Common
King's Lynn
East Winch Common
Walton Common.
R NAR
Pentney
Narborough
Marham Fen
Swaffham
R OUSE
Whissonett
Horningtoft
Briston
Rawhall
Lexham
Honeypot Wood
Hoe Rough
East Dereham
Hockering
Scarning Fen
Lolly Moor
R TUD
R WENSUM
Foxley Wood
Reepham
Cawston
Booton Common
Buxton Heath
Swannington
Felthorpe
Blickling
Aylsham
North Walsham
Felmingham
Westwick
R ANT
Dilham + Smallburgh
Barton Broad
Alderfen Broad
Stalham
R THURNE
How Hill
Ludham Marshes
Hoveton
Belaugh Broad
Thurne
Filby Broad
Burgh Common
Acle
Stokesby
Cockshoot Broad
Ranworth Broad
Upton Fen
THE BROADS
Norwich
R YARE
Wheatfen + Surlingham
Strumpshaw
Buckenham Broad
Cringleford
Fritton Lake
Haddiscoe
Reedham
Howe
R CHET
Brooke Wood
Saxlingham
Woodton
Topcroft
Hedenham
R WAVENEY
Beccles
Flixton Decoy
Lowestoft
Oulton Broad + Carlton Marshes
Barnby Broad
Pakefield
Kessingland
Denton
Alburgh
Flixton
The Ilketshals
Gissing Common
New Buckenham Common
Old Buckenham
R TAS
Hethel
Hingham
Seamere
Lower Wood, Ashwellthorpe
Watton
Wayland Wood
Griston
Merton
Thompson Common
Little Cressingham
R WISSEY
BRECKLAND
Beachamwell
Caldecote
Foulden Common
Cranwich
Mundford
Great Hockham
Snetterton
Eccles
Langmere
Ringmere
Fowlmere
Devil's Punchbowl
Santon Downham
Fellwell
Emily's Wood
Weeting Castle
Weeting Heath
Washes